IN PRAISE OF *Life Lessons in Success*

I am so proud of this group of authors – I was there the day they made the commitment to create this book. Not only did I present each of them with their Certified Trainer Canfield Methodology diploma but I have come to know all of them as individuals who are willing to push forward with their goals. They share a commitment to being of service and helping others to achieve their best. I believe their stories will help you do just that.

Patty Aubery, #1 New York Times Bestselling Author *Chicken Soup for the Soul,* Creator of Permission Granted, GoalFriends CVO President, Jack Canfield Companies

I am thrilled to endorse *Life Lessons in Success.* I have personally worked with every author in this book, and each of them has a unique and inspirational story of being human, breaking through setbacks, and stepping into their potential.

Stories have the power to inspire and connect us as humans. This book will do just that! These stories are real, relevant, and have the power to transform!

Kathleen Seeley, Founder, Massively Human Leadership

I happily endorse *Life Lessons in Success*. I know Angie Dobransky through our mutual love of BCS Mexico and our shared vision of helping others by sharing our stories and wisdom. She and her fellow authors share their personal stories to inspire and connect with all who take the time to read them. These stories will make you laugh and make you cry and show you the ability we all have to overcome any obstacle to live lives full of joy, success, and human connection.

    Chip Conley, Rebel Hotelier

    New York Times Bestselling Author

I've always said that an idea without action is just air. In life and in business, one must have a healthy dose of idealism and pragmatism in order to achieve a certain level of success. You have to do whatever it takes to get the job done. Angie's book serves as a reminder that sometimes we have to go back to basics in order to get back on track. Nothing wrong with starting over. Hard work does pay off!

    Jeffrey Hayzlett, Primetime TV & Podcast Host, Speaker, Author, and Part-Time Cowboy

LIFE
LESSONS
IN
SUCCESS

WISDOM TO WIN THE GAME OF LIFE

Published by: Capucia, LLC
211 Pauline Drive #513
York, PA 17402

Paperback ISBN: 978-1-954920-02-6
eBook ISBN: 978-1-954920-03-3
Library of Congress Control Number: 2021905067

Cover Design: Ranilo Cabo
Layout: Ranilo Cabo
Editor and Proofreader: Simon Whaley
Book Midwife: Carrie Jareed

Printed in the United States of America

TABLE OF CONTENTS

FOREWORD

In 2019, sixty people from all over the world came together to participate in my live Train the Trainer Success Principles certification program. I have made it my life's work to research, understand, and then teach the principles of success and the practical strategies and disciplines that operationalize them. These Success Principles are the proven principles that the world's top achievers live and operate by, that allow them to excel in their careers, finances, relationships, and all other aspects of their life.

These sixty people came from all over the world, and for some, English was not their first language. Their backgrounds were as varied as the colors of the rainbow. Levels of income and wealth ranged from just starting out to multi-millionaires. There were men and women, young and not-so-young. Some were religious; some were not. Business owners, employees, retirees, consultants, coaches, professionals, and the unemployed all found they shared a common link—a desire for experiencing more fulfillment and impact in life and the willingness to learn.

Although I created the space for the magic to happen, these five-dozen people from all walks of life quickly formed a deep bond by sharing very personal stories of failures and successes, dreams dashed and dreams realized. The unifying theme was that each of them had leveraged all their life experiences to learn, grow, and continue to evolve. They supported and encouraged each other as they learned new skills and shared their stories, and a powerful community was formed.

The intensive training to learn the Canfield Methodology took place over an entire year, with Zoom calls each month and two separate seven-day weeks spent together in live training sessions in California. The participants met for the first time in April, not knowing what to expect. Each had a mix of anxiety, excited anticipation, and tempered optimism about what they were going to experience and the challenges they would have to overcome to successfully graduate.

After the first week, they all went home to continue their lives, fulfill assignments for the training, and continue the monthly Zoom calls. During this time, each student had to spread their wings, leave their comfort zones, and start putting their new learnings into action. We reconvened in October in Palm Springs. There the transformational experience continued, and the participants faced the challenge of standing on stage and presenting the Success Principles with interactive exercises to their peers and to me.

As the group connected and shared their stories, they did not want their positive, focused, and inspiring time together to end. So on the last day, one of the participants asked for a few minutes to present an idea to the group. Angie Dobransky suggested that the group write a book together to continue their collaboration and to share their inspirational stories with the world.

That was the birth of the idea for this book, and I could not be more proud of the group for how they have worked together over the months to collaborate and refine their stories. The result is the book you now hold in your hands, in which I am sure you will find not only inspiration but also practical insights on how you can overcome the obstacles and challenges in your life, so that you too can achieve your dreams and create a thriving and fulfilling life.

My dream is to have one million trainers around the world sharing and teaching the Success Principles so that the whole world can live in peace, harmony, and prosperity. These new trainers are helping me realize that dream as they incorporate the Success Principles into their lives and their work.

The authors have included their biographical and contact information at the end of each of their stories. When a particular story resonates with you, I encourage you to reach out to them and let them know.

If you'd like to learn more about becoming a Certified Canfield Success Principles Trainer, you can learn more at our website www. jackcanfield.com.

Jack Canfield
New York Times bestselling author of the *Chicken Soup for the Soul*® series, *The Success Principles*™, and *The Success Principles Workbook*

INTRODUCTION

In life, often we invest time, effort, and money into a project or opportunity for some very specific goal or to solve a defined problem or issue. We usually consider the investment of energy worthwhile if the process produces the results we were promised or if we at least learned something valuable along the way. Sometimes, those investments produce results far above and beyond what we could have ever envisioned when we initially set out on the journey. That is what happened for the authors of this book.

Each author in this collection is a Certified Canfield Trainer in the Success Principles and a Certified Canfield Trainer in the Canfield Methodology. We have committed to living The Success Principles, and most of us are also committed to teaching them through our skills and talents. We have chosen stories from our own lives that taught us these valuable lessons and helped us grow. We share them with you to connect, inspire, support and encourage, and, to keep us bound to each other, sharing our stories and living our lives to their fullest success.

As you read our stories, there are a couple of concepts that flow throughout and are bedrock principles for living a life of purpose, passion, joy, and success. The first of these is

$$E + R = O$$

Event plus Response equals Outcome

Events happen and may be beyond our control, but our response is up to us. Different responses bring different outcomes, and successful people vary their responses to get the desired outcome.

Changing our response leads to the second fundamental principle. To achieve ones' highest success, we must

Take 100% Responsibility

for our responses and, therefore, for our results. No matter the event, we always have the option to choose a response in support of our dreams rather than react. It is not always easy to accept that we are responsible for everything we do or do not have in our lives, but once we do, we gain the power to make change where needed.

Finally, a simple formula that supports the bedrock principles is

BE X DO = HAVE

Whatever we have in life is a result of who we are and what we do with our responses. Sometimes we need to change our actions to improve our results. Sometimes we need to change ourselves.

We are excited to share our *Life Lessons in Success* with you. As you read our stories, in whatever order you choose, we invite you to share both our tears and our joy. And, we hope we can help you achieve success.

Thank you for sharing our journey, and we wish you much success!

Event

+

Response

=

Outcome

ACTIONS SPEAK LOUDER THAN DREAMS

by Angie Dobransky

"The path to success is to take massive determined action."
— Tony Robbins

When I was in grade two, my teacher told me that I was smart and that through education I could have anything I wanted from life. I believed her and declared that I would be a college graduate. The seed was planted.

This wasn't an easy choice. My parents owned a small, two-bedroom house and my father worked as a letter carrier. My mother was a housewife who had a small typing business to make ends meet. They agreed that going to college was important, however, they would not be able to support me financially. Not only did I have to get accepted to college, but I also had to find a way to pay for it. I took action and found myself a part-time job at a shoe store and started to save my money. I applied to college and was accepted; the first step was completed. I asked my manager if they could give me full-time work and accommodate my class schedule the following year. They agreed. Two weeks before school started, I moved into a small inexpensive apartment, and for the next four years, I worked a minimum forty-eight-hour, retail job managing a shoe store while also taking a fifteen-hour class load and earning the 3.85 GPA so I could be accepted into the business school in my junior year. I did it, got my college degree, and landed a job in the exciting world of retail fashion.

The first time I flew on a plane was for a work trip, and I was terrified, pretending not to act like it in front of others who were more traveled. I worked hard, used my skills, and climbed the corporate ladder. I traveled regularly for work and pleasure, seeing much of the US and visiting exotic lands for vacation. My hard work and dedication paid off. I was successful, living exactly the life I had imagined when I was young.

At forty-three, I was a single mother with a son I adored, a rewarding and exciting career in the fashion industry, first as a department store buyer and then an account executive and sales manager for several big-name brands. I owned my own home on a nice piece of land. I bought a new car every four years. I took two or three trips to cool places for vacation each year and had the ability to do and purchase almost anything I wanted. My wants weren't that great, but I certainly wanted more than my fair share of great shoes! I was very comfortable and fulfilled, for a while. I came from humble beginnings, and I had ridden the American dream from lower-middle-class beginnings to a wonderful place.

I was in my early forties and had reached a level of comfort in my life, but as time went on, I found myself becoming slowly, yet steadily less satisfied and unhappy. Looking back, I realized all my life had been goal-oriented and now that my goals were fulfilled, I didn't really have a direction. Changes were happening in the fashion industry and the next positions up the ladder did not appeal to me. I became restless, knowing that I needed to make some changes and explore what I wanted to do next. Then I got the call: my father had a hemorrhagic stroke. The initial call from the hospital told me he was unlikely to survive. I flew down to Florida immediately. My father started to improve, however, he would need support, and it would take weeks of rehabilitation for him to recover. I decided to take an eleven-week leave of absence from my job to support my father.

When I returned from my leave one of the first things my boss said to me was, "I want you to know we were really surprised at the choice you made." I had put my family before the company. I knew at that moment, I had to make a change. I had to take action. I knew that I could do anything I put my mind to. After all, I had never really failed at anything I set out to do. So, eventually, I quit my job. It was time to take action. I never really saw it as a risk, so confident I was in my own ability.

I started my business in August 2007, because it seemed like the perfect time to start a business. The market was on fire, everyone was making money, and opportunities were everywhere. I was the single mother with a teenage son, with a mortgage and sole responsibility for keeping us both afloat. I quit my salaried corporate job, bought a coaching franchise, and started my own business. I was disciplined, hard-working and dedicated, and ready to set the world on fire as a business coach. I had real-world experience on a large scale and a coaching model that had been used to support thousands of small businesses. I never entertained any thoughts of failure.

Anyone who has ever started a business, particularly as a consultant, coach, or service provider, knows how hard that first year can be. It was much harder than I anticipated. It took me four months to sign my first client, but I wasn't particularly concerned. Many things I dove into in life were harder than anticipated, but I figured out how to do them and moved forward. *Be X Do = Have* worked in my life long before I learned the formula. I figured out what I wanted, asked what needed to be done to get it, and became the person I needed to be to take those actions. I had done well in business, and I had plenty of savings and investments to get me through until I could turn a profit.

The market peaked on October 9, 2007, just two months after I started my business. Over a span of seventeen months into the spring of 2009 the Dow Jones Industrial Average dropped 54%. On September 16, 2008, the failures of massive financial institutions in the US caused a global financial crisis. The great recession hit. Half of my investments disappeared in forty-eight hours. Half of what remained was frozen in a brokerage account by the federal government. They were trying to prevent market free fall, and this meant that I was unable to access that cash that I needed and had counted on for many months. In retrospect, there probably was not a worse time to start a business.

In the summer of 2009, my son was a sixteen-year-old junior in high school. He had plans to fulfill his dream of being a chef by attending Johnson and Wales University. I left my twenty-year career and started a business just before the recession, thinking it would be a huge success. The credit of most small business owners had been cut off. Sales had dropped dramatically and, while many of them wanted coaching, finding those who could also pay for coaching had been very difficult. By August 2009 I had no money left in the bank, my son's college fund was gone, and my investments had been liquidated to keep us going. And I reached a point where I did not have next month's mortgage payment in the bank.

I was terrified, desperate, angry, ashamed, and embarrassed. I didn't know what to do. I didn't know how I was going to pay the mortgage, feed my son, and keep us going. And I certainly had no idea how I was going to pay the $40,000-year college tuition that was coming in just two years.

I just kept thinking, how am I going to tell my son that we have to move? That I lost the house? That there's no money for school? That I failed him, failed our family, and failed myself? I had paid for my college education by working a full-time job while attending school, and I wanted to do better for my son. I always encouraged his dreams. I wanted him to be everything he could be. I was willing to support him no matter what that took, and yet now I had failed and there was no money for the mortgage and certainly no money for his college.

I knew that only I could change this situation. $E + R = O$ had always been a theme in my life. I would get myself into situations, over my head, and determine my response to reach my desired outcome. I knew that I had to take action to make a difference. So, in my darkest moment, I rose up, and I decided that I would call ten business owners every day, five days a week, for thirty days. It was a frightening thing to make those calls, but the fear of failure was even greater, so I executed that plan and in September 2009 I earned $16,000. That was more than enough to pay the mortgage, and my business started to completely turn around. I learned that day. We are always in control of our results and doing nothing determines our results until we act. To this day, whenever I need more clients, I pick up the phone, take action, and start calling ten people every day.

Another lesson I learned through this experience is that even when we know what to do, we don't always do it. Had I called ten business owners every single day from day one, my business would have never been struggling in the first place. After all, we live in a time where even if we don't know what to do, exploring Google and YouTube we can find almost any instruction manual we need. Successful people do whatever they need to do, take the actions they need to take, thus ensuring they receive the outcomes they desire. All of us can have anything we want when we simply take action and take 100% responsibility for those actions.

Now my life is comfortable again. My business is successful, and I can afford almost everything I want. My son finished college and is working in a restaurant. I remarried and we are planning our next big adventure, building a retreat center in Baja California, Mexico.

Angie Dobransky is an award-winning coach, trainer, and speaker who shows people how to reach RADical success by applying The Success System to their lives and businesses. She runs transformational retreats where people uncover their vision and create a plan to live a life of passion, purpose, joy, and success. Through coaching, workshops, keynotes, and training sessions, she works with individuals and companies to grow people to their fullest potential. Her one-to-one coaching pushes people to be their best selves. Learn more and find free resources at www.RADStrategic. com. Or, reach out directly to angiedobransky@radstrategic.com

THE POWER OF ASKING

By Amy Burton

"Asking questions is one of the fundamental keys of learning. It is always better to ask a question than pretend you understand."
— Catherine Pulsifer

Growing up, I was a curious little girl with a zest for life and a keen sense of awareness. I was observant and outspoken, a "girly girl" who loved to play with dolls, yet as bold and brave as any rough-and-tumble boy in the neighborhood. I was happy and carefree, willing to take risks, and always ready to stand up for what I believed in. Even in the midst of chaos, regardless of how scary things got, I had a deep sense of calm within. Hidden beneath the surface of my fearless nature was an uncanny inner knowing. I learned at a young age to follow my intuition. Even when others disagreed or thought my ideas were crazy, I trusted my instincts.

My mother was soft-spoken and beautiful, a gentle woman who cared for her family with the inner strength of a mighty warrior. My father was handsome and forceful, a guy who had a knack for getting what he wanted. They separated a few years after my younger brother was born, divorcing while I was still in elementary school. Growing up in a broken home came with some challenges, but it wasn't that bad; in fact, if my parents had stayed together, I wouldn't be the person I am today. My inquisitive nature sometimes irritates others, especially those with less prying minds, but that has never stopped me from asking questions. When I make up my mind to do something, I usually find a way to make it happen.

As a teenager, I harbored a lot of anger toward my father. I had questions that were never answered, a heart that needed healing, and the pain of betrayal that wouldn't go away. I had little tolerance for people who hid behind facades, something which still bothers me to this day. There was ugliness living in my soul. Unresolved issues from my childhood silently haunted me, but I was desperate to find a way to let my light shine.

In my sophomore year of high school, I learned about a cosmetology course being offered in our junior and senior years. The thought of making people look and feel beautiful was so appealing to me, I didn't hesitate to enroll. Although my mother was supportive, my father and my guidance counselor argued I was too smart to be a hairstylist, encouraging me to attend college in pursuit of a more prestigious career. I was a bit discouraged, thinking maybe they were right, but my intuition guided me to press on. Somehow, I knew this career path was the right choice for me.

I graduated from high school in 1981 with a skill that launched my career at the age of seventeen. I spent the next fifteen years making people look and feel beautiful, just as I had imagined doing in my sophomore year. I had a wonderful opportunity to touch multiple lives on a deep level. I met so many interesting people. I learned more during my first year in the salon than some people learn attending four years of college. I loved my job. I was an excellent stylist and had a lot of fun serving my guests.

After getting married, as our little family grew, I cut back my hours to spend more time at home with my two sons. Desiring additional income to offset the time away from the salon, I asked myself how I could turn sewing, something I loved to do, into another source of income. We didn't have the luxury of Google back then, so the fastest way to find answers was to ask someone. I contacted a client who designed and fabricated custom wedding gowns. Although dressmaking was the farthest thing from my mind, I instinctively knew she was the person I needed to speak to. Within minutes she had me connected with a networking group filled with entrepreneurs who were sewing for a living. New friends, new questions, and new adventures were waiting!

My curiosity and tenacious nature opened doors I never thought possible. My initial desire to earn a little extra income from home turned into a multi-faceted, fifteen-year career in the custom drapery industry. Whenever an idea came to mind or a new opportunity presented itself, I dove in and found someone to ask – how, what, when, why – I used the answers to create new opportunities for myself. Before long, I found myself writing course curriculum, teaching hands-on classes, speaking at conferences, traveling around the country presenting seminars, writing articles for international trade publications, filming instructional training videos, and finally working in research and development for a large distributor in that industry. All of these amazing advances in my career happened because I followed my intuition, fearlessly asked questions, believed the answers were waiting, and took massive action!

Then in 2008, as the economy crashed and the entire country was consumed with fear, my career in the drapery industry came to a screeching halt. My sons, one a senior in high school and the other in eighth grade at the time, were old enough to understand the devastating toll a job loss could have on a family. I sensed their anxiety as I delivered the news. Thankfully, my husband, John, encouraged me and held our family together as we rode out the storm. Always believing everything is really happening "for us" instead of "to us," I knew, in the end, we would be stronger, so I forged on.

Pondering my next move, I thought back to the recession of 1981. I remembered when I was working as a hairstylist my income was not affected by the downturn in the economy. I honestly never thought I would go back to working in a salon. My body was now much older and definitely out of shape. The thought of standing behind a chair again was less than appealing, but when times are tough, we carry on. After taking a job in a local salon, life was finally settling back down. Then one sunny morning while working alone, two uniformed employees from the power company came in to shut off the electricity. Here I was, working for someone who couldn't even keep the lights on! Not only was I embarrassed for the owner, but my guest was also so uncomfortable, she never returned. Concerned and upset, I knew it was time to move on.

Shortly thereafter, during a morning ride to school, my son Jake suggested I open my own salon. I immediately dismissed the idea as ridiculous. My first thoughts were – absolutely not – it's too much work, I don't have any money, the economy is weak, we'll never make it…and besides, I haven't a clue how to run a salon! Sure, I can handle anything when it comes to hair, but own and operate a full-blown salon with employees, no way! Anxious and a little afraid, with few options ahead, I began feeling that familiar entrepreneurial spirit tugging on my heart once again. I stopped the crazy chatter long enough to ask myself why I was filling my head with all the reasons why I didn't want to do this. The idea was insane yet intriguing at the same time. I began asking myself, if I did open a salon as Jake suggested, how could I impact the lives of others? I envisioned owning a company that would not only make people look and feel beautiful on the outside, it would inspire and empower them to shine on the inside as well.

I knew I had to find someone, somewhere, who owned and operated a successful salon so I could find out how to do the same. After a few phone calls, I hit the jackpot! I contacted a salon owner a few hours away and offered to take her to dinner. Before I knew what was happening, she was flooding me with incredible information. In addition to the wonderful resources she shared, she cautioned me to hold off for a few more years. She didn't think I had enough clientele or enough money to open a nice salon just yet. Against her advice, I followed my intuition, took the information she shared, and ran with it. I made phone call after phone call, asking so many questions my head was spinning. The more I inquired, the more I learned. I stepped out in faith, following the whispers of that still small voice, guiding me to carry on.

In April 2011, the doors to my new company, Revel Salon and Color Studio, opened in Lake Wylie, South Carolina, with just one employee – me. Every year since, our company has thrived and grown tremendously. We continue to uphold and support our vision to inspire and empower young women; we have created an incredible culture. Our company is blessed beyond measure with an amazing team of talented women who encourage and lift each other up daily. I am so grateful for every one of them, and for the continuous support of our loyal guests.

Of course, it has taken a lot of hard work and dedication to come this far. We have faced many hurdles over the years, some of them seemingly insurmountable at the time. Through it all I have held onto the belief that following my intuition, believing anything is possible, asking questions, and taking action always produces massive success. This belief has brought me farther than I ever imagined possible. When I was laid off all those years ago, if someone had asked me what I would be doing in ten years, I never would have guessed I'd be doing what I am today.

Someone once told me – "You are either green and growing or ripe and rotting, but never standing still."

Over the years, I have continued to keep the momentum going, always in a forward motion. I am excited to see what the future holds. I have several new ventures underway, all of which would not be possible had I not followed the whispers of my soul, asked numerous questions, believed in endless possibilities, and taken action.

If my father were here today, he would be so proud of my accomplishments. My mother, now in her eighties, is as beautiful as ever. She is my inspiration and the source of my own inner strength. Her fearless courage taught me invaluable life lessons. Although I never heard her speak these words, I instinctively learned, it is often through pain and heartache that we discover our true inner voices. Mom showed me that pushing past what brings us sorrow reveals beauty in the ashes. In order to overcome obstacles, we must dive deep within ourselves, for it is there we hear the whispers of our souls. It is there we claim the magical power hidden within each of us.

I am grateful for both of my parents and their love for me, for their vast differences, and for the pieces of each of them I have carried with me throughout my life. Despite the obstacles I have faced, I have found that same resilient inner strength my mother modeled for me and combined it with the boldness and tenacity my father demonstrated. I speak my mind and stand up for what I believe in. I trust my curious nature, understand the power of asking questions, and continue to fuel my success with tremendous vision and action!

I encourage each of you reading this story to remember this:

"Every question asked is an opportunity for growth. Curiosity fuels creativity – trust your intuition, learn to practice the art of asking, then follow up with action."

— Amy Burton

Amy Burton is a thriving business owner with a diverse entrepreneurial background. Her million-dollar company, Revel Salon and Color Studio, is located in Lake Wylie, South Carolina. She is an author, a certified Canfield Success Principles trainer/speaker/coach, a certified RIM® facilitator, a Barrett certified consultant, and a sales mastery coach. Amy is a board member of Rise Together International, Inc., a nonprofit organization bringing hope and healing to impoverished families. Throughout her career, Amy has continued inspiring and empowering ordinary people to live extraordinary lives. To learn more about Amy and the services she offers, visit: www.AmyABurton.com

Using the Law of Attraction to Manifest My Dream

By Grace Liang

"We become what we think about all day long."
— Ralph Waldo Emerson
"What you radiate outward in your thoughts, feelings, mental
pictures, and words, you attract into your life."
— Catherine Ponder

English is my second language, so when I first read the words "Law of Attraction," I initially assumed that this principle was all about how to be an attractive person to others! I now have a much better understanding of this principle and believe in it wholeheartedly. I live by this principle, and I am amazed by the wonderful results it has produced for me.

Shortly after I lost my husband to cancer about three years ago, I searched the Internet wanting to know what happens to a person's soul after they die and if I would ever see my husband's soul again. After watching many YouTube videos (some were fascinating, while others were quite strange), I came upon the movie called *The Secret* and this is where I discovered the Law of Attraction. This is also where I encountered the book *The Success Principles* by Jack Canfield. Both of these events have changed my life.

If you are not familiar with the Law of Attraction, it essentially states that "What you think about, talk about, believe strongly about, and feel intensely about, you will bring about." I had always been a very action-oriented person who believed only hard work could bring me what I wanted, along with a bit of luck! Based on my forty-plus years as a human being, the actual results seemed to vary. When I first learned about the Law of Attraction I had a lot of mixed feelings about it. On the one hand, I was excited to learn about this brand-new concept, but on the other, I was a bit skeptical. Could someone simply think about what they wanted, believe they could get what they wanted, and it would just magically happen? That just sounds way too easy, right?

Becoming a published author has been one of my dreams since I was in middle school. Like many people though, life got in the way and most of the time I was doing my best just to survive. Once I turned forty, my life was finally in a good place, and I was able to settle down. I met my soulmate, married him, left China, and moved to America. I learned another language (English), earned my teaching certificate, and became a full-time teacher. During this time, I was able to focus on my passion for writing again and started to write about my love for fashion, beauty, and travel on my blog.

During the fall of 2016, which was about seven months after my husband's diagnosis, I started sharing our journey of fighting his cancer on my blog. All of these posts were popular and I received many comments, messages, and emails from my readers. They thanked me for sharing because it helped them see some hope and light, even in the darkest times of their lives. After my husband's death in 2017, I continued to write about my journey on how I was able to turn my life around, and how I have grown from surviving to thriving. During this time, many people suggested I should write a book about my story to help more people, so that is exactly what I did.

Writing the book was not the hardest part because the words seemed to pour out of my head and heart with ease. However, finding someone to publish the book was very difficult. I attempted to go the traditional route and find a publisher on my own, but that didn't go anywhere. At one point, I was going to self-publish on Amazon, but deep in my heart, I wanted to find a publisher so I could become a true, published author. During this time, I had also started learning about the importance of affirmations. I wrote out a few of my own, just to give it a try. One of those affirmations was to become a published author. I would spend a minute or two just daydreaming about the moment when I saw my book at the bookstore, visualizing it in my mind. I imagined what I would wear to my book launch party and then imagined the moment when everyone congratulates me!

In late April 2019, I flew to California for a seminar. While waiting to board my flight, I was called to the customer services desk and told that I had been upgraded to a Comfort seat. What? Cool! It must be my lucky day! While talking to the airline staff at the customer service desk, I noticed a middle-aged lady next to me.

She was shaking and seemed like she had been crying. I felt my heart ache for her, but at the time I was not sure what I could do to help her. After boarding the plane, I settled into my Comfort seat and was waiting to stand up for the other person who had the window seat to arrive. A few minutes later, the middle-aged lady that I had noticed earlier came in and sat in the seat next to me. We said hi to each other and then settled into our seats. Suddenly, she leaned over and whispered in my ear, "Please forgive me for bothering you, but I hope I don't scare you later if you see me crying. I just went through some personal life changes and I am still trying to process it." I assured her that she was not troubling me at all and we waited for the flight to take off.

Once we were in the air, I turned on my computer and worked on doing some final edits to my book. The lady sitting next to me would either stare through the window next to her or would check her phone and would then cry. Feeling her pain, I decided to talk to her and we both shared our stories. I learned her name was Tracy and, during that five-hour flight, we created a deep bond. I was so glad to see her eyes light up again! When Tracy and I said goodbye at the LAX airport, we hugged over and over again and exchanged phone numbers to keep in touch.

Right before we went our separate ways, Tracy suddenly asked, "I noticed that you were working on a book earlier. Have you found a publisher yet?"

"Not yet," I answered.

A big smile spread across her face and she said, "I am a publisher and I would love to publish your book." From that moment on, the rest is history!

Fast forward to today, my book *Finding Grace: How to Navigate the Journey from Tragedy to Triumph* is published and in bookstores and online. This book recently hit #1 on Amazon's Hot New Releases list and also made it to the top 100 in four categories. Tracy and I also became good friends, and I'm planning to write my second book. Thanks to the powerful Law of Attraction I had the perfect publisher come into my life and she helped me make my life-long dream of becoming a published author come true!

This is just one of the many wonderful results that have occurred in my life thanks to using the Law of Attraction. After learning and practicing this principle for about two years, here are a few tips on how to use it in your daily life:

- The Law of Attraction perfectly matches up with what I have learned over the past year about taking 100% responsibility for my life. To do so, understand that we came into this world to enjoy the journey and to also create our reality. Everything that we experience in our life, good or bad, is under our control.
- The Law of Attraction doesn't act against your actions. This principle only adds on an extra action, which is to imagine the ideal results that we want over and over in our head.
- Practice your affirmations (some people call it daydreaming, lol!) twice daily for about ten to fifteen minutes total. Usually, it takes about sixty-eight seconds to activate a thought into energy, and the more time that you can spend doing this, the more likely you can attract what you want into your life quickly.

Are you ready to attract your ideal life to your reality?

Grace Liang is a speaker, certified trainer for Canfield Success Principles, certified practitioner for Emotion Code, and #1 New Release Amazon Best Selling Author of Finding Grace: How to navigate the journey from tragedy to triumph. Grace's personal story of living her dream life after overcoming poverty, family abuse, domestic violence, moving to a foreign country, and losing her husband to cancer will bring you hope and inspire you to thrive! She focuses on teaching people how to Live Gracefully inside and out so we can all enjoy a fulfilled life have it all (peace, love, health, wealth, and perfect self-expression). You can follow her Facebook page, Living Gracefully, or visit her website https://www.activateyourinnerpower.com to learn more!

FROM BULLIED TO EMPOWERED

By Jeannette Paxia

"Our prime purpose in this life is to help others.
And if you can't help them, at least don't hurt them."
— Dalai Lama

My big brown eyes looked up at my father. Our deep brown eyes were a family trait; in fact, when you looked at pictures of our family, all you would see were brown eyes. This time my brown eyes were full of tears. I looked up at my dad with dismay. Crying was a daily occurrence at this point, as every single day I begged my parents to please let me stay home from school. I had started a new school in third grade a couple of years before because my parents didn't like the way our public schools were changing. They felt sure the classes were not challenging enough and that my learning was being delayed as a result. Reviewing the options, my parents thought sending me to a Catholic school would change all of that. Little did they know what was going to happen. Although I was intellectually stimulated at my new school, I was bullied. Every single day.

When I started as a new student, the first thing the other students did was ask me what my parents did for a living. Everyone wore uniforms, so kids couldn't tell which families were wealthy or poor based on clothes. Unfortunately, my shoes still gave me away. I was an extremely honest child, perhaps to a fault. So, as soon as they asked me where I got my shoes, I quickly and proudly answered, "Kmart." I had no idea that Kmart was a store that would be looked down upon. I had never dealt with anything like this in public school. When they then asked what my dad did for a living, I proudly told them. I was so proud of my father. He had immigrated to this country knowing only two words of English, with a seventh-grade education. When he found himself unable to continue school, he learned English by himself and then supported his whole family by working hard as a forklift driver. I saw him working hard seven days a week, twelve hours a day to support and provide for our family. In my eyes, we were rich. I felt we had everything we needed. I knew that my parents paid for everything in cash. We always had food. We had a roof overhead, and we even had a swimming pool. To the children at my new school though, we weren't wealthy. Their parents were lawyers and doctors, who had a great deal more money than we had. Looking back now, I'm glad for my innocence. I didn't realize the difference between our classes.

I quickly found myself the person that was bullied by everyone. If I went to the bathroom, the bullies would follow me in and corner me. They would make fun of me. Sometimes they would hit me.

When I went to the playground, they would corner me there and make fun of me, hit or kick me. To say that I hated going to school was an understatement. I would cry and beg every single day for my parents to change my school or keep me home. Anything, so that I didn't have to go to school.

I found no refuge at school. Even my teachers seemed to join in, making fun of me when I wouldn't participate in an activity we had to do for class. When we read the book *How to Eat Fried Worms*, they decided that after we finished the book, we would fry worms and eat them ourselves. As a child who didn't even like meat, I couldn't imagine eating a worm! I chose not to participate. I got physically sick even thinking about eating a worm. My teacher made light of my decision not to participate. I failed the assignment. Grades were important to me, so failing only made me feel worse about myself. This same teacher was my teacher again in the fifth grade, and for the entire year, she called me Jennifer instead of Jeannette. She couldn't even bother to get my name right.

One day, a new girl started at our school. I was happy as I figured this was my chance to make a new friend. Her parents, like mine, weren't that wealthy, so we had something in common. For the first few days, we were the best of friends, as I stood by her, showed her around, and made her feel welcome. This didn't last long, as the children who were bullying me, decided they would befriend her. They didn't want to be her friend, but they really didn't want me to have any friends. It worked, and she would no longer hang out with me. At this point, I felt like the entire class was bullying me.

I was getting more and more depressed as each day progressed. I would walk into the school, head down, tears in my eyes. Every day I lived in fear. I had to will my body to move, just to walk in the school. I constantly looked behind me and was aware of everything going on around me. I was afraid to go into the bathroom, or anywhere that I knew I could be cornered.

I knew my parents supported me, and that was one of the only things that kept me going. My parents tried to go to the school administration, but no one would help. My mom and dad felt that the school wasn't responding or helping because we couldn't afford to financially donate or support the school beyond tuition. School tuition was hard for my parents to come up with as it was, so donating any extra money was not something they could do.

To this day, one of the happiest days of my life was when my parents told me I could change schools. When it became clear that the school administration wouldn't do anything to help, my parents knew it was time to make a change.

On my last day at that school, I walked in with my head held high, happy that I would never have to step foot into class with these kids again. That was the day that I decided that I would do whatever I could to make sure others didn't suffer the way I had. I wanted to help children who were bullied, to provide them with whatever they needed to feel safe. I knew I never wanted to see another child cry every day like I had.

This is my story and it has made me who I am today, so I wouldn't trade it for anything. When I was in high school, I became friends with a few of the people who had bullied me. I asked them why they had done it, they said because they wanted to go along with everyone else and didn't want to be bullied themselves.

I am now a transformational speaker, coach, and children's book author. My passion is working with children and teaching them the tools they need to increase their self-esteem. My biggest reward is seeing children embrace the information and apply it to their lives. I believe that a child who is self-confident doesn't allow other children to define them. If I had felt better about myself all those years ago, nothing those kids said to me would have mattered. If I hadn't cried and begged them to stop, they likely would have left me alone. The reaction they got from me is what kept them coming back for more. Before attending that school, I had been at the top of my class and popular. I had never had anyone treat me the way I was treated there, so I reacted the only way I knew how. Now I help children by providing them with tools that I didn't have. I believe this is our collective duty. Together, we can stop bullying. By educating children and their parents, we can make sure that everyone has the chance to learn in a safe environment, where they don't feel less than others, and where they are free to be themselves.

Jeannette Paxia: For as long as she can remember, the basis of Jeannette's life has been, what can she do today to change the world? As a transformational speaker and coach, she's passionate about helping everyone live the life that they want to live, no matter what age they are. She is also a children's author. Her You ARE a Superhero book and anti-bullying program will not only guide children to find their unique qualities but will also engage adults. Jeannette has a way of engaging the audience and providing them with the tools they need to increase their confidence to change their lives. Learn more about Jeannette at https://paxcoach.com or https://youareasuperhero.net.

Seeing Your Best Life When the Worst Comes

By Hanna Hermanson

"Imagination is everything.
It is the preview of life's coming attractions."
—attributed to Albert Einstein

There I was, in my tiny apartment in the heart of San Francisco, sitting on the dirty wood floor. I stared at five red Rubbermaid containers stacked in the corner of the room.

My palms were clammy. I felt heat building in my body. Were my ears ringing? All I could hear was my heart pounding inside my chest. My mind raced.

This is crazy. This is never going to work. Everyone back home was right. I was foolish and naive to think I could come out here and make something of myself. I should have known better.

I downsized my entire Midwestern life into those five plastic containers to move to San Francisco. The nice apartment I had in Madison, Wisconsin, and the steady government job, were now just fond memories.

Why did I completely uproot my life? I had accepted a position working for a promising startup to bring yoga to schools in California. The dream of West Coast living, the invigorating ocean air, and no more bone-chilling, snowy Wisconsin winters, were too much to ignore. I had clear visions of working in sunny coffee shops and seeing the huge smiles on teachers' and students' faces after I said, "namaste," in their classrooms. I was about to do the work I love, with people I admired. I was about to manifest my purpose in the most thrilling city in California.

But as my dad always told me, "Things don't always go as planned, kiddo."

Just a few weeks after I made the big move, my new dream life derailed. My gut dropped as they delivered the news. In a walking meeting with the CFO, I heard the words I never saw coming—

"Actually Hanna, we can't afford you. You don't have a job with us. But enjoy San Francisco."

I had worked hard to get on-boarded for a few weeks. I was already teaching classes, and the schools were expressing their gratitude for the yoga.

That familiar feeling of clammy palms, heat rising in my body, and racing thoughts set in. I stopped hearing what the CFO was saying to me. All I could think was, "No way. No way I'm letting this happen. No way they are doing this to me. No way they can't afford me."

I did the only thing I could think of. I rolled out my yoga mat. The visions I had for myself succeeding in California were still clearly in the forefront of my mind. I still saw myself working in sunny coffee shops, living my purpose, and doing work that meant something to me.

Yet here I was, in one of the most expensive cities in America, jobless, friendless, and sharing my tiny space with five big Rubbermaid containers at the end of my yoga mat. Reminders of my *old life*.

What if I just went back home? I could probably get my old job back. See my friends and family. Probably have to endure some "told you so" comments, but I would be back in my comfort zone.

I knew I had to pull myself together. Chasing a dream doesn't mean buckling at the first signs of adversity. I owed it to myself to try.

I'm going to figure this out, I told myself. I have this apartment and my laptop. I'll give myself a year to figure it out. To see where life takes me.

Back in Wisconsin, I had been an academic advisor. I loved helping people realize their potential. Maybe it was time to take a closer look at my own potential.

The months after being laid off were filled with a lot of personal development. I read books and downloaded worksheets. I went to vegan retreats and yoga classes and absorbed information from anyone I could sit down in front of. I discovered ways others became successful and tried to learn from their stories.

A few weeks later, a Success Trainer was hosting a workshop nearby. What did I have to lose? I went—the trainer talked about the power of visualization and encouraged everyone to make a vision board. Again, nothing to lose, right? So, I even spent a long afternoon creating a vision board. I searched through countless internet images of places I wanted to go, things I wanted to do, anything that represented who I wanted to be. I collected scenes of train rides through the mountains, women meditating on grassy hills, and crowds of people coming to see me speak – and accept my offer of coaching.

After I found a bunch of images that resonated with me, I walked to the FedEx store to get them all printed in color. It cost $16, and, at the time, I wondered if it was a sound investment.

I thought about getting a frame for my vision board, but I knew it would be another expense I should probably do without, given the current balance of my bank account (dwindling).

As luck would have it, I found a frame on the street while walking home. For free! Was it just luck or did I manifest it? In hindsight, I think it was the latter. Either way, you bet I picked it up and slapped my dream life cut-outs into the matting!

After completing my vision board, I put it on my desk. I sat at that desk, for many more months, working to integrate all I learned about success to set up my own coaching business. All the while, this art-and-craft project was the background of my workspace.

The next eighteen months were a roller coaster. As anyone starting a business can tell you, it's filled with little successes and big setbacks that aren't for the faint of heart.

I kept going. At first, it wasn't easy. As that vision board collected dust, I gained fifteen pounds, went into debt, and put a strain on all my family relationships. At some point, my roommate asked me to put the vision board away. Another item for the Rubbermaid containers.

I kept telling myself, if it's meant to be, it's up to me.

The small successes got a little bigger. My business grew. Eventually, we moved into a slightly larger apartment. During the move, I once again found the vision board. Since we had a little more space, I hung it up on a wall near where I worked.

I remained focused. I asked for help. I connected with mentors and masterminds to help me figure out how to reach my financial goals. And I had some really good months. Sure, the lean months still haunted me from time to time, but the good was starting to outweigh the bad.

About eighteen months after my life turned upside down, my partner and I sat in a brewery. We always wanted to explore the world while living in our backpacks. Since my business was doing well and I could easily work remotely, we began to realize this was more than just a dream. We could make it a reality.

Here I was again. Packing up with those Rubbermaid containers. This time on an exciting journey with a promising future. While packing the vision board, I took a closer look.

I couldn't believe it.

As I looked at the pictures I'd printed out what seemed like a lifetime ago, I discovered most of those visions were realized.

I spoke in front of students. I took an amazing train ride through the mountains. I had women calling about my coaching services. There were people saying and understanding, "My dream life is my real life." And now, to my excitement, I was packing up to travel the world and meditate on grassy hills.

You see, I was too busy working hard and being caught up in financial goals to celebrate the successes realized on my vision board. And, actually, I think that was a missed opportunity. If I would have acknowledged my successes along the way, would the journey have been easier? Less stressful?

I guess if I had any regrets during this time, being too busy to acknowledge my successes would be at the top of my list.

So how did the vision board help me? After all, it pretty much sat in the background – or in a container – without me giving it much thought.

But maybe it was that tool working in the background – helping my subconscious mind troubleshoot and achieve goals.

Visualization is an important way to create the life you want. It stirs up your creative powers, focuses your brain, and attracts you to people, resources, and opportunities you need to achieve your goals.

Visualization helps activate the Law of Attraction – the most powerful law in the universe – in your favor. This law states that whatever you focus on you will attract into your life. Whatever you are thinking and feeling, is ultimately the request you send out to the universe.

Basically, every single moment, what you see and think about is what you bring about.

It's easy to do. In fact, if you just close your eyes and see your goals already complete, you're activating your subconscious mind. Visualize with all of your senses. What does your dream look like, sound like, even taste like? How will you feel when you accomplish your goals? The more details you put into your vision, the more real it becomes.

Sure, it won't happen all at once. You will have to get to work.

When you set clear goals, have a vivid vision, and take steps each day to realize this vision, the universe tends to give you a little help along the way. Maybe it is an opportunity you didn't expect or running into a person who could eventually be a trusted resource. You just have to be open to the help the universe offers.

Some people have trouble visualizing. As much as they try to picture their goals realized, the images don't come easily. This is when a vision board can be especially helpful. Finding images that correlate with your personal goals can be an everyday reminder of what is important in your future life.

As Albert Einstein once said, "Imagination is everything. It is the preview of life's coming attractions."

So, what coming attractions do you want to see for your future self? Close your eyes and start visualizing them.

Hanna Hermanson is a certified business coach and success trainer, helping coaches and entrepreneurs build brands that afford them freedom. She lives her philosophy of "Dream Life is Real Life" and is continually working to create more streams of income, contribution, and purpose for herself and her clients. You can find her work in Forbes, YouTube, Amazon books, and of course her website: www.dreamlifeisreallife.com.

Rejection's Antidote

By Melissa J. Shea

"Love conquers all."—*Eclogue X*, Virgil

It started like so many other real estate closings, where my husband and I were buying a distressed home. As we walked in, we greeted our attorney with a hug and kiss. I then noticed the seller's attorney was someone we knew as well, and gave him a hug and kiss, too. I also was happy to see the realtor, title closer, and bank attorney again. It felt like a high school reunion seeing old friends. As we were catching up, I noticed the seller and could sense his discomfort and dread. I walked over, sat next to him, reached out my hand, and looked into his eyes.

"Miquel, how are you feeling? I am so glad you're here," I said, compassionately.

"I'm okay. I just want this all to be over," he replied.

"It will be soon, and when it is done, you will breathe a huge sigh of relief and your new life can begin," I said, still holding his hand.

I could tell he knew what I meant and somehow without saying it, he realized I was once in his shoes. Miquel smiled back and squeezed my hand. As we spoke, my goal was to ease his fears, while respecting his dignity.

"I appreciate everything you've done for me," Miguel said. "But, why do you do this type of work? What got you started?" he asked, intensely.

This caught me off guard. The best answer I could quickly give was a clichéd response, "I was once in your shoes."

Miguel lost his job a year prior and faced homelessness due to the impending foreclosure. Most people in this situation have family to stay with. That wasn't Miguel's case. His only living family was a distant cousin in another state. My company helps distressed homeowners secure a new residence, assists in mitigating foreclosures and home sales. In this successful case, Miquel was walking away debt-free, with a new place to live, and a check for $10,000. We also enrolled him in a credit rehabilitation program to repair his damaged credit.

I said, "Tonight is going to be the first night of many that you're finally going to get a good night's sleep. I'm very happy for you." From his expression, I could tell that he knew I meant it. He breathed a sigh of relief and his stress began to lift.

I returned to my assigned seat next to my attorney, and the closing began. I started reflecting on Miguel's question. Why do I do this, and what got me started? It was so much more than the cliché answer. I chuckled to myself, reflecting on how today I purchase homes as often as people buy clothes. Which is in stark contrast to the time I lived in my Jeep for three weeks, begging friends and family just to let me stay a night. I started to reflect on how I became homeless and more importantly, how I transitioned to the place I am today.

My thoughts took me back to 1986, the week after Thanksgiving. I was twelve and my two sisters were eleven and eight. Our parents sat us down and told us that we would no longer be celebrating Christmas. After that statement, there was silence as my sisters and I processed this news.

"Why?" I finally said, sheepishly.

My parents explained that Christmas wasn't Jesus' birthday, instead, its roots were in Pagan traditions. I had no idea what that meant. They may as well have been speaking a foreign language. We were in shock but managed to mutter out a few more questions as tears ran down our faces.

"Is that for just this year or forever?" my sister asked.

"No, we will no longer be celebrating any holidays again," my dad replied as a matter of fact.

"Did we do something wrong?" I asked.

"No," my mom answered. "It's just that we want to please God, and this is what He wants us to do. You do want to make God happy, don't you?" She asked in a tone that I knew not to answer back. Of course, we wanted to please God, so the three of us nodded. Tears continued.

It wasn't the absence of presents I was upset about, it was missing celebrating with my aunts, grandparents, and especially my close cousins.

That moment set a path for our family that we'd never return from. Over the next few months, we were *love-bombed* by people from this congregation. Members showered us with extraordinary attention and an overwhelming illusion of love. We drifted further from our aunts, grandparents, and cousins. It was years before I would see them again.

I remember that first Christmas, sitting and looking out of the window, when my Aunt Donna came to our house. She had two big bags of presents. My mother yelled from the window that we weren't celebrating Christmas and to keep the gifts. My aunt insisted that she'd didn't have receipts to return them. My mom insisted we could not accept the gifts and we haven't any gifts that Christmas.

I stared at my aunt as she walked away with a confused and angry look on her face. One that I'll never forget.

Over the following years, we lost connection to people we'd had loving, long-term relationships with. My best friend at the time, Krista, lost her father that year and I had to tell her that we could no longer be friends. I was only allowed to have friendships with people who had the same beliefs as my parents.

Some would describe this as a cult. The way we spoke, the things we did, and the people we saw, all changed without us children really knowing what was happening. All actions were to "please God" and this religion was telling us how. At the age of twenty-two, I had married someone in this same faith through an arranged marriage, and after a miscarriage, I began questioning everything. Why did the miscarriage happen? Why couldn't we celebrate birthdays, listen to certain music, or go to college? The reply of the elders was that I should know better. I was deeply depressed due to the miscarriage, being married to someone I didn't love, and my faith's limitations. I felt so alone. Nothing made sense and all I kept doing was questioning, "Why, why, why?"

My questioning led to the worst punishment in this faith. Shunning—a complete cut off from all family members, friends, and the community. Suddenly, I would walk into grocery stores and people who have known me for years, had stayed at my house, and I did missionary work with, would look the other way when they saw me. It was cruel and unloving taught behavior.

My sisters also no longer had anything to do with me. My parents disowned me. They even went so far as to tell me it was my fault and if I repented, they would talk to me again. In order to do that, I had to go through the painful process of being reinstated which took the minimum of a year.

I was in a rage for years after the shunning. I tried three times for reinstatement, begging and pleading, but the community would not show any mercy. I felt betrayed, lied to and so angry at the religion and my parents. To make matters worse, my husband filed for divorce.

Shunning is the harshest form of punishment, in my experience. It is meant to manipulate and control others, to force them into thinking and behaving the way the group wants. I understand then that God could never be part of that religion because God is love and this sanctioned activity was anything but loving.

The next two years were extremely difficult. When you leave this community, you are told that you'll be murdered, raped, or killed because you are no longer under God's protection. For a year, I lived in absolute fear. I spoke to no one unless I absolutely had to. I barely went to work. I made no friends. I was afraid of everyone. I was forced to live in a world where I knew no one and didn't know how to speak to so-called worldly people. I only spoke of the Bible and the terminology of the religion.

Prior to my shunning, I was living in my mother-in-law's home, but because my husband filed for divorce, I had to leave. I stood at my parent's doorstep and begged to stay there, just until I could feel safe. They said no. I had tears in my eyes, telling them that I was afraid for my life. I'll never forget my dad saying, "No," and slowly shutting the door. My heart sank and I wept for days.

I had no money and nowhere to go. I lived in my Jeep for the next three weeks until I could get a small apartment. The loneliness and stress left me depressed and hopeless, leading to an attempt to take my life. It was the week of Thanksgiving. I drove past my parent's house for what I thought would be the last time, then carefully wrote a suicide note, drank a full bottle of wine, swallowed over fifty aspirin, and all the other pills I found in my medicine cabinet.

By some miracle, I woke up four days later soiled in my bed, with what I can only describe as the worst hangover ever. The most devastating fact was there was not one message on the answering machine; no one had knocked on my door; no one found the note; no one took me to a doctor. I sat on the edge of my bed and realized that if I had left this earth, no one would have noticed.

That was the day I changed my life. I had been given a second chance and I decided that when I actually died, someone will notice. I decided to call my Aunt Joanne and asked to celebrate Christmas with the family. She cried tears of joy, and if she could've leaped through the phone she would have. That Christmas was the best day I could remember being reunited with all my aunts, uncles, and cousins who showered me with kindness. No one judged me; no punishment just unconditional love.

That was when I started to heal. I forgave the religion for misleading so many people, my parents for putting religion before God and family. I forgave my sisters and former friends. All of them rejected me, but I learned to overcome that with love. I found that if you forgive those who hurt you, the person who benefits most is you. You can't change others; you can only change yourself. The antidote to rejection is love because love conquers all.

These thoughts were interrupted when someone at the closing table asked me a question and I quickly returned to the matter at hand. I glanced over at Miguel, and now had the deeper answer to his question. I do this work because of love for others, especially those who are suffering. If I can help spare the pain of abandonment and rejection, and the fear of homelessness, then I am not living in vain. I am living in love.

Melissa Shea lives on Long Island, NY with her husband John and is the mother of eight beautiful children. She is the president of LIREIA (Long Island Real Estate Investor Association) and Everyday Funding and Everyday Realty Services. Her companies work to help foreclosure prevention, homeless prevention, and renovate distressed homes in the community. She is a public speaker and transformational coach to educate others to become financially independent through real estate. Connect with Melissa at www.lireia.com.

LEAN INTO YOUR DREAM

By Carole B Young

"You don't have to be great to start,
but you have to start to be great."
—Zig Ziglar

Stories come in many shapes, sizes, and forms: books, movies, documentaries, or a quick personal share between friends, just to name a few. The emotional and physical impact can change someone's life forever. For most people, watching a great movie or sitting down with a good novel is the easiest way to download a fiction or nonfiction experience into the mind. The best part about a novel or motion picture is not having to think about what comes next, but just waiting with anticipation to see how the story will twist and turn before concluding with a happy, sad, or unexpected ending. I love getting lost in a good story at the movie house while snacking on chocolate, popcorn, and soda. Have you ever been watching a movie or listening to a story and put yourself front and center, imagining that it was you? If we were to be honest with ourselves, we would agree that often we all live through the experiences of others—at least once in our lives. In my mind, I realize that every day I am writing my own story even while watching that cool flick on the big screen.

Have you ever had a dream for your life: an imagined event where your most treasured desires all fall into place and you are living the life of true happiness? I believe that some of the best stories start with a dream. This could be a dream you have while sleeping or while daydreaming when you have a few moments of silence in your busy day. For years, I would have daydreams about writing a book that becomes a box office hit movie. I still have this dream today and have so much fun visualizing how it has made it to the big screen and I am accepting the Oscar on stage for "most inspirational film." When I come back down from the clouds, I feel like it would be a very big mountain to climb and generally move on to another thought, or my daydream gets interrupted by life that always seems too busy to focus on these kinds of dreams. Truth is, every good accomplishment starts with a thought or a dream.

A little over eighteen months ago, I had the opportunity to share my story in my own chapter of a book. This was a book series that included inspirational stories of women who were willing to share their triumphs over difficult times or being blessed with a miracle. When I was first presented the opportunity, I had a really difficult time believing that anyone would be interested in hearing about little ole me. I had shared my story during a strategy session with the main author of the book series and she assured me that it was an amazing story. In the back of my mind, I felt that it was not enough to intrigue the readers. I had a choice at this point. I either decide to write my chapter, or not! The fear that I was feeling was real, and that feeling in the pit of my stomach of stepping into unchartered waters without a life jacket was terrifying to me.

Guess what? I decided to just LEAN INTO IT! What does that mean, you ask? I said to myself, *Just go for it!* Even though I had never done anything like this before, I just started writing. The whole time I was writing, I was battling with the negative thoughts and self-talk that my story was not good enough, or I was experiencing Imposter Syndrome. An article in the Harvard Business Review ("Overcoming Imposter Syndrome" by Gill Corkindale[1]) states that Imposter Syndrome can be defined as, "a collection of feelings of inadequacy that persist despite evident success." I would write then delete, write then delete, over and over again. About half-way through, I realized that I had a pretty interesting and different childhood than most. I mean, how many books do you read where the writer was one who grew up in the carnival business? My parents owned an amusement company that traveled the US. My learning experiences were priceless and my dad was the best in teaching business. I was a very lucky girl, but some did not see it this way. I never shared my past because I was concerned about being judged by others. So while I was LEANING INTO IT, I was battling the thoughts of not measuring up, self-doubt and self-sabotage. I powered through it! As each word built the paragraph, my momentum increased at warp speed.

It took about two months to write what was to be about a ten-page chapter. This was my first experience of officially writing for a

1   https://hbr.org/2008/05/overcoming-imposter-syndrome

book project. Thank goodness for the book editor fixing the grammar mistakes and changing it to allow the reader to flow through it gracefully. Then came the time for the book to be published and launched. We were told to market on social media and reach out to friends and family for support. To my surprise, I was elated with all of the support I received. I felt I wasn't an imposter after all. I was doing this and I was feeling pretty amazing! The book went on to become a #1 International bestseller on Amazon. I was so excited and it felt such an accomplishment!

I learned so much about myself during this time of writing and stepping out of my comfort zone. Instead of sitting on the sidelines procrastinating, deliberating on whether or not I was qualified to do it or even contemplating possible failure, I said to myself, "Carole, just *Lean Into It*. Just start." Even though I had no idea what the outcome would be, I allowed myself to be open to the opportunity, without a promise of success and any expectation. I had not always been this brave. It all started about five years ago.

It was in August 2014 that I was introduced to personal development. I attended a Breakthrough to Success (BTS) workshop with Jack Canfield. I returned home with a whole new outlook and was a sponge for more. I read books, watched videos of Jim Rohn, Bob Proctor, Les Brown, and of course, any material from Jack Canfield (my favorite). I understood everything but believed I was just not good enough to do something that would have a positive impact on others. Before taking on this book project, I struggled with what my purpose in life was. By *Leaning Into It*, I have discovered my true passion all along has been helping others, mentally and physically.

I recently completed an intense one-year training program with Jack Canfield, to become certified as a trainer and coach in the Success Principles and Canfield Methodology. My dreams and goals are now bigger than EVER before! I want the same for you!

I truly encourage you to dream big and just *Lean Into It*, whatever *It* is, big or small. You see, we have to begin to finish. I believe that God created all human beings with different talents and spiritual gifts. We have a special and unique footprint for a reason. Where will you make your impact?

I challenge you to evaluate your life and determine the areas that you would like to improve or start anew. Make a list and decide on just ONE task or goal to start with. When deciding to make a change or start something new, we must pair it with integrity. Integrity is the inner sense of wholeness from qualities, such as honesty and consistency of character. Never give up! You cannot fail if you don't try it!

Just *Lean Into It*. Just start!

Carole lives life gracefully with intentional purpose. She stands firm on the God-given spiritual strengths of belief and courage. Working with businesses in the financial payment services industry for over twenty years, Carole decided on a course correction. She now shares her expertise in multiple areas: business culture diagnostics and value discovery, trainer/educator of leadership programs and personal development, transformational speaker, business consultant, senior consultant at The Alzheimer's Advisor. Reach your peak, transform your company culture, create transformation in your life, or find and define your IT factor. Contact Carole B Young at cbyAchieve@gmail.com.

Don't Believe Everything You Think

By Cindy Hochart

"Bad news is that you can control nothing but your thoughts. Good news is that with your thoughts you can control everything else."
—Debasish Mridha

Although I grew up in a financially and emotionally poor and dysfunctional family, I was blessed with intelligence, a drive for achievement, and a default positive attitude. By any measure, my life has been blessed. By the time I was fifty years old, I had achieved upper-middle class work success with happy well-adjusted children and a thirty-year marriage to a man I still loved and respected. I was a Registered Nurse with an MBA, a certification as a Project Management Professional, and extensive experience in developing innovative health care programs, building and leading teams in hospital systems, technology companies, and health plans. I was earning $150,000 per year and had an impressive resume of skills and experience.

However, these accomplishments were achieved despite many failures and bumps in the road that in hindsight might have been warning signs for impending disaster. Between 2002 and 2012, I changed jobs five times. In each case, I told myself I was moving up – getting more money, more responsibility, and more experience that would make my value to employers even greater. All those things are true, but the default positive attitude I was born with and my level of happiness were on an insidious decline. The job I left in 2002 ended five years of award-winning performance as Director of Population Health in a health plan. It was an involuntary termination that I told myself was due to the unfairness and capricious nature of corporate America. However, in truth, I was very unhappy and it showed up on the job in how I handled conflict. That's a story for another book. I got another, bigger, more prestigious job within thirty days as a Vice President of Care Management. Although I loved the job, my staff, my boss, and I contributed to the company's awards and achievements, I left within two years for a more national opportunity.

The cycle repeated until I found myself working for a start-up software company developing a way for behavioral health care providers to better integrate physical and behavioral care for their patients. The company's headquarters were in New York City. I was living in South Texas and my client implementation site was in Seattle. As a result, I was away from home nearly every week. When in Seattle, I worked long hours meeting with providers and traveling with people that I did not know very well. When in New York I arrived to work before anyone else but most staff arrived late and worked late. I was emotionally and physically exhausted, which led to an episode of acute back pain while in New York City. After seeking help at a local urgent care center, I spent two days in the hotel, alone and in pain. When I returned to the office, my boss took me into a stairway for a private conference. (The stairwell was the only privacy available in the open loft configuration of the office.) This man is the reason I agreed to work in this high-risk start-up company. I had worked with him before, had huge respect for him, and was honored and proud that he recruited me to join his team. On this day, however, he told me that he was concerned about my performance. The actual job performance and outcomes were not the issue. The problem was that he received feedback from the senior psychiatric staff that I wasn't a good fit with the team. I was reportedly stand-offish and aloof. He suggested that I spend more time with the team and get to know them. Go out for drinks with them, invite them out for dinner, "show them the Cindy I know." As I sat there in the stairwell, trying to visualize working up the energy to wage a "like-me" campaign with the staff, I just couldn't do it. The phrase, "I got nuthin," was never more true.

I gathered my things and went to the airport for my flight back to Texas. That flight was one of the longest in my life. I sat at the back of the plane in row 38C with tears running down my face. I seemed to be completely invisible to everyone around me as I sat there in my misery. For the duration of the flight, I sat there replaying how badly I had messed up my life. I told myself that I was worthless, damaged, broken; that I had a repeating pattern of screwing up relationships; that I wasn't smart enough, pretty enough, popular enough, and just didn't have what it takes to be successful. I started visualizing opening up the airplane door and jumping out, anything to end the pain. It was right there - less than ten feet away. I could open the door and be out before anyone could stop me and it would all be over. I could visualize the freedom and relief. I would no longer have the pain in my chest that was crushing me. I would no longer have to worry about how to make enough money to support myself and my family because I would be gone. My family would miss me, but they would be better off without me dragging them down.

Since I am here, writing this book, I obviously did not proceed with opening the door. You probably also know there are numerous safeguards in place that would not have allowed me to successfully open the door anyway. If I had tried, that would be a story with more drama, but what actually happened was the plane landed and I got off. What came of it though, was a realization that I had to make a change. If I was at a place of self-destruction, I obviously needed to rethink the path I was on. The next day I resigned from my job with no plan for doing anything more than figuring out a new path and begin to heal. After a few weeks, I purchased a program from Steve Harrison and Jack Canfield called *The Bestseller Blueprint* to help me learn the process of writing and publishing my first book, which I had always wanted to do. Through that process, I published *Find Your Burning Bush, Discover God's Plan for Your Life*, and was exposed to *The Success Principles* by Jack Canfield.

The most foundational of the Success Principles is to take 100 percent accountability for your life. Canfield teaches that people act as if everything they experience is a result of their own behaviors, thoughts, and images that they hold in their heads. I have always known I control and am accountable for my behaviors, which explains why I am a *doer* and a high achiever, but for my thoughts and images? That idea was revolutionary for my life. The very notion that you can choose to be happy based on what thoughts and images you focus on was akin to learning a new language and just as hard to accomplish. But more astounding still is the fact that your success in all avenues of life, including financial and relationships, are a direct result of the stories you tell yourself, about yourself and about the world. When I was sitting on that plane, telling myself how worthless I was and visualizing plummeting to the end, I was only contributing to my own cycle of misery and, through the law of attraction, bringing more of the same into my future. I acknowledge in retrospect that I was emotionally and physically exhausted, which is often referred to as burnout. However, the real cause of the physical and emotional symptoms was not understanding and taking accountability for my cesspool thought patterns. I blamed former bosses, the broken health care system, my employees and peers, my parents, and my husband. I could expound at length about the epidemic of poor management existing in corporate America. Underneath it all, I blamed myself for not being good enough, popular enough, influential enough, pretty enough, and enough-enough to be successful and happy.

Over time, with continuing training and practice, I have substantially rewired my "stinkin' thinkin'" and now choose my future by choosing the thoughts and the images I visualize. I have become more aware of the limiting beliefs I have held as universal truths. Beliefs are nothing more than thoughts you have experienced over and over until they become an unconscious foundation for decision-making. Those beliefs drive all of your outcomes including financial results, relationships, and the impact you have on the world.

Patty Aubrey, President of Self-Esteem Seminars and my coach and mentor, says that if you are going to make up stories to tell yourself, they might as well be good ones that propel you forward rather than hold you back. I continue to work through and resolve limiting-beliefs as I become aware of them. I now consciously decide what I want for my future and surround myself with people who support my goals and my vision of who I am and what I want to contribute to the world. Today, I have a successful consulting company that makes a positive impact on American health care and the people who work there. I have a network of like-minded positive friends and associates that enrich my life. I also have a loving husband of forty years, four children, and eleven grandchildren that I love expansively and unconditionally. More important than all of that, I have decided that I love and believe in myself and am grateful for all the gifts I have been given. In fact, it is this more than anything else that represents the fundamental transformation of my life of misery to one of joy and love. It all starts and ends with the thoughts and images I allow myself to focus on. It's not just about accepting, but loving yourself and rejecting any limiting stories or beliefs that do not contribute to your happiness and to you having everything you want from life. Transforming your underlying belief system (your thoughts) will transform your outward reality in every way that is important.

Cindy Hochart, President of On Fire Outcomes is a transformational consultant working with individuals and teams to achieve On-Fire results in cost, quality, and satisfaction through assessment, transformational training, and leadership development. Cindy has thirty years of experience developing high-performance teams and is an author, an accomplished health care consultant, a registered nurse, and certified project management professional. Cindy is also certified in a number of tools used in helping her customers such as Barrett Values Assessment, and Canfield Training Methodology. Visit www.onfireoutcomes.com to learn more or connect with Cindy at cindy.hochart@onfireoutcomes.com.

GRIEF CHANGES YOU: FIND YOUR TRIBE

By Samantha Ruth

"Surround yourself with people who add value to your life.
Who challenge you to be greater than you were yesterday.
Who sprinkle magic into your existence just like you to do theirs.
Life isn't meant to be done alone. Find your tribe and journey freely
and loyally together."
— Alex Elle

Grief changes you, in so many ways. From my overall life perspective to my hobbies, I'm just not the same person anymore.

I've learned to accept that. I don't know that the rest of the world accepts that—and I accept that, too. Grief also teaches you more than you ever asked to learn.

It didn't happen quickly or easily, but it happened—and that's what's important. At first, I resisted it, trying to get back to being the Sam I was before my world was shattered.

The outside world wanted this Sam back, too. Whether people compared my mood, my health, my appearance, it didn't matter. I was always being compared in some way. Even by myself. Especially by myself.

I've been insanely hard on myself my entire life. Even as a child. This self-judgment didn't come from parents or teachers. It came from within. Unrealistic expectations and such high standards were just how I was wired. I was always striving for perfection, and always disappointing myself—not anyone else, just me.

I felt like I was never good enough. That is until I met Jim. He had this way of making everything difficult disappear. I could get lost in his eyes and his smile. He brought the best out in me. We brought the best out in each other.

We met when I was twenty-four and he was twenty-six. We were just babies! Our connection was unreal, instant, and magical. Without even trying, he helped me treat myself with kindness. He helped me see myself through his eyes.

My dad reminds me of this pretty frequently—that I've always been at my best when I'm with Jim. He's my person. My soulmate. My absolute one and only. And I knew that from the beginning.

I've always marched to the beat of my own drum. Not everybody gets me. I wasn't ever picked on or bullied but I always felt different. Like I didn't completely belong. Admittedly, much of it was my own doing as I didn't want to *fit in*. If it was trendy, I wanted nothing to do with it. But I still felt out of place. Until I met Jim.

We started taking interfaith marital classes together, planning a future. But we both had lots of growing up to do and were so focused on our careers. So we went our separate ways.

The result was that we were both devastated. I think we knew that we belonged together. Yet, we also knew that we had more of living life on our own to do before we could be together successfully.

But I was a mess. I was lost. All those personal insecurities that melted away while we were together came back in a flash.

So, I threw myself into my work. It was a pivotal time in my career that really catapulted me to the next level. And it wouldn't have happened if we stayed together. Jim moved from Michigan to Colorado and made the most amazing life and career for himself.

When we reconnected more than ten years after breaking up, we picked up exactly where we left off. We knew life together and we had known life apart, so we cherished every moment together.

We were engaged five months later and I moved from Michigan to Colorado two months after that. I was happier than I ever believed was possible. I was thrilled to be planning our wedding, which was 1000% for Jim. I wanted to elope, and now I am so thankful that we didn't. We had the most incredible wedding weekend in the mountains with our dearest friends and family. It was everything.

We had everything. My insecurities again melted away and we were living the life of our dreams. We were planning our future, not taking each other for granted because we knew what it was like to be apart. However, I took time for granted. I thought we had all the time in the world. While I absolutely cherished every single moment, I just assumed we'd have a million more.

It was three years, four months, and eleven days after we got married that Jim collapsed at work, unable to be revived, and my world was blown into a million pieces. How is that even close to enough time? We found our way back to each other only to be ripped apart again.

I had so many thoughts like this, only to instantly feel guilty for having them. I honestly just survived. I just barely functioned with family and friends guiding me because I was utterly lost. I felt like a helpless child again. Grief changes you.

I questioned myself. I agonized over every decision. I beat myself up for not being the same Sam I'd always been, for learning differently. I used to read things once and remember them forever. Studying was a breeze. Now, I read the same sentence a dozen times before processing it. A standard set of instructions can take me days to understand. Don't even get me started about things that have always been difficult. Grief changes you.

There are triggers for my grief absolutely everywhere. A perfectly good day can turn into sobbing in an instant. These events derailed me for the first year without Jim. It rocked my world, in a miserable way and it still does—for a snippet of time, and then I plow forward again.

The first clear moment I remember having is about seven months after he passed and I was thinking about our upcoming fourth wedding anniversary. I wanted to continue our tradition of going to the spot where we got married.

My loved ones were against me going to the mountains alone. I know they were just worried about me. The childhood version of Sam, the Sam who took care of everyone else, always—that Sam—probably would have listened because thinking about what I want isn't something I'd done very much of in my life. I spent time taking care of everyone else, without even giving a thought to taking care of myself. Grief changes you.

I suddenly didn't care what anyone thought. For the first time in my life, probably. Perhaps it was Jim guiding me, seeing the best in me, wanting the best for me. Or maybe it was just my intuition. Instead of questioning myself, which I'd done plenty of before, I listened. As a result, I had one of the most pivotal weeks of my life.

I met someone who connected me with my mentor, Jack Canfield, and his training programs. I signed up for all things Jack and made a decision to devote 2019 to myself and my healing.

This is something I never would have done for myself in the past. I wouldn't have done it even if Jim was still here, frankly. I take care of everyone else, putting myself last, right? This was the complete opposite: making myself the priority, with no other plan. No other end goal. And I had to just let go of all of that. I had to get comfortable being uncomfortable. I had to lean into not having everything mapped out. I had to learn to see the clues, to embrace change, and to listen to myself—like I did when I went to the mountains!

And just like going to the mountains, this has proven to be another one of my best decisions. I connected with my tribe. Jim is my soulmate, and much like he brought out the best in me, so does my tribe. They get me. This me, without comparison. They helped me see the beauty I wasn't capable of seeing. They helped me believe—in myself, in life, and in my ability to heal. This is actually something Jack teaches, although he calls it surrounding yourself with successful people. I call it finding my tribe!

Just by making the decision to take care of myself and to devote 2019 to myself and my healing, I began to create the life I'm living now. I didn't know how it would happen, and that was truly difficult. I was not at all great at embracing change—and I did it anyway.

I'm still living a life sentence I never asked for. I still cry every day. Emotional triggers still trip me up. However, now they don't derail me for hours or days anymore. I don't bounce back like I once did. And that's ok.

There are good things in life—things we celebrate, like fulfilling a lifelong dream of becoming an international best-selling author. That's something to celebrate! I still burst into tears. Yes, I absolutely felt the joy, but I just as profoundly felt Jim's absence. I know he was watching, so very proud. But it's a moment I wanted to celebrate together, and it reminded me of all the moments I'll have, wishing he's here by my side. Laughter, or any moment of happiness, is now followed by this sense of pain and panic. It passes, but it happens. Grief changes you.

But now I have my tribe to help me see how far I've come. Believe me, I still have so much farther to go, but for once, I can also see how far I've come. That's a big deal, an especially big deal for me.

Earlier this week I was watching the series finale of *Criminal Minds* and sobbing. Yes, you read that correctly. I was sobbing at *Criminal Minds*. It doesn't make any sense, I know. Except that it makes perfect sense.

When Jim came to Michigan to help me pack and move to Colorado, he made fun of my obsession with the show. It was a miserable Michigan winter, and while I was at work, wouldn't you know Jim somehow got hooked on *Criminal Minds*! It became one of our things to do together.

The ending of the show was rather fitting—as characters who have passed away came back to talk with current characters, I couldn't help but feel like it was a sign from Jim, coming back to talk to me. And as much as I talked about being this New Sam who needed to get back those missing pieces of myself, my tribe helped me see that they never really left.

Grief changes you. In so many ways. From my overall life perspective to my hobbies, I'm just not the same person anymore. I'm a better one. Because I let go and embraced change, because I surrounded myself with the very best souls, I found my way out of the darkness.

So whatever darkness you're facing, don't face it alone. Let the right people in. Let go of the toxic ones. Find your tribe. Even if it feels completely out of your comfort zone, give it a chance. Embrace the changes you're afraid of. Your life will change, in ways you never even imagined.

Samantha Ruth is a transformational speaker, psychologist, and coach. She helps people by guiding them to live their best life—as their true self. She has the tools and heart-centered teachings, not only based on her education but from her own life experiences. She has had her world shattered into millions of pieces and come out on the other side, stronger and on a mission to help others put their pieces back together. If other methods or professionals didn't work for you, contact Samantha and see how you can pick up your pieces and get Un-puzzled—together. Learn more about Samantha at www.samantharuth.com or connect with her directly via email: sam@samantharuth.com.

The Present – Living Life's Greatest Adventures

By Pam Miller

"I don't want to sit and wait to die. I want to live until I die."
— JJ Bouma

Life, for me, was waking up every morning with a sense of completeness. My life had some twists and turns; some good, and some I learned not to repeat. I had been a single parent for six years when JJ and I married, creating a new family with four children, two boys, and two girls—all of them teenagers! Blending them into a new family could have been difficult, but JJ and I fully embraced the challenge—and each other. I count my blessings to have had a husband who, when I said, "I love you," always said, "I love you more."

We loved being together, creating fun and adventures wherever we went. One evening, we all went out to dinner. We walked into a restaurant, and one of the children put our name in for a table of six. Then when the hostess announced, "Bradys, party of six," the children and other people waiting laughed out loud as we all walked towards the table. A great sense of humor was shared by all the kids. During the children's teenage years, the respect they had for each other was terrific; we felt so fortunate when we heard different stories about blended-family problems. Don't get me wrong; there were spats on occasion. However, forgiveness and kindness were what JJ and I always tried to model when they had disputes. The children knew deep down that they were loved by all their parents, step or not. JJ and I united as parents, to show our children what unconditional love felt like. We continually showed them what a successful marriage looked like, as well.

When we had been together ten years, JJ started to have a scratchy voice and cough after a severe cold around Christmastime. Up until then, he was never sick—in fact, he was one of the healthiest people I had ever met. So off we went to the doctors to get his symptoms checked out. After several months of no answers, our doctor ordered a CAT scan and EEG muscle testing. At the appointed time, we walked back into the doctor's office to hear the results and treatment plan that would finally get him better. The doctor walked into the room with a very somber demeanor. We wondered why, but soon heard the unbelievable words: "JJ, I'm very sorry to say you have a diagnosis of ALS." At that moment, the air sucked out of the room, and I found I had no breath. We looked at each other and knew what it meant—a death sentence. We had watched our pastor struggle with ALS for five years before he retired from the pulpit, and the daughter of an employee in JJ's company was battling the disease. So, we knew what we were facing.

There was nothing to say to the doctor, so I just listened, but I felt like I was in a very long dark tunnel hearing voices from way far away. The doctor was telling us to go home and be with our family and friends and share this news of "no known cause" and "no known treatment to extend your life" with our loved ones. Our future was gone. All our dreams were gone. We had planned to travel and spend time at our vacation home, boating and snow skiing with the family in northern Michigan. We had planned to savor together the fun of watching our grandchildren grow up. But it felt as if our future had evaporated into nothingness.

The only clear thoughts I had, nudged me to begin focusing on how we were going to handle JJ's challenges—a vibrant, loving, and successful businessman, husband, father, and grandfather who was only fifty-three years old, now faced with inevitable decline. I searched deep within me how I would support and love him through the next two years, that we hoped he had left.

We left the doctor's office, and JJ threw me the keys to the car and said, "You drive." As I slid into the driver seat, I placed my hands on the steering wheel to stop them from shaking. Looking up at the bright blue sky, I silently said, "OK, God, this one is too big. I need your help." JJ and I both had a solid faith. It was what truly brought us together. Now, I drew on this faith like never before.

"Where do you want me to drive?" My voice cracked asking the question.

"Go to the lake," was his answer.

My in-laws lived on Lake Michigan, so I headed there first to share our news. Shock and great concern were on both their faces and we knew it would take time to process. Then we continued on to visit our children. JJ needed to be with them and to console them. Even then, he comforted everyone with his signature line, "Everything will be OK." We then continued to call on our extended family and friends throughout the weekend to share the news. It was hard for everyone to accept, including us! In disbelief, we grasped at straws and looked for a different diagnosis. We decided to contact the Mayo Clinic for a second opinion the following week.

Waiting for the next appointment, we both felt exhausted. We were, I think, on autopilot. But I realized that while we had talked with everyone else, yet we had not talked about us. My heart was crying out: *What about us?* I had a sense that JJ needed to be the one to start the conversation, so I waited. Our turn finally came on the evening when we returned home from sharing our news with so many. Sitting in his favorite chair, staring at the television straight ahead in silence, he then spoke.

"I don't want to sit and wait to die. I want to live my life until I die."

The flood gates finally opened up! We held each other and sobbed our hearts out. It was the defining moment for us. We shared every thought we had ever wished we had said but had left unsaid. We found the place of knowing that, no matter what, you have each other's back. We were in this together, and we each knew it was going to be the greatest adventure of our lives and not just an ending of a story.

JJ was CEO of a family-owned commercial construction company. Monday morning came, and a meeting was scheduled for all employees to attend. JJ stood firm, explaining his future, and courageously stepped down from daily operations. I stood by his side, and he squeezed my hand while telling everyone in the room, "My life is on warp speed now, wish me well!" There was great applause, with tears streaming down so many faces. JJ was loved and respected by so many!

JJ was a big thinker, and adventure was his middle name. Previously, we had built two orphanages in Albania when the country left a communistic regime—then hosted Albanian businesspeople in our home in the United States. Wherever there was a call to help others, we always opened our doors.

Now it was time to plan the year that was ahead of us. We went to the Holy Land and climbed mountains. We took all of our children, their spouses, and grandchildren to a tropical island to create more memories in the sun. We bought a red Corvette convertible and made plans to drive on Route 66 across America. A group of our friends said, "Let's all go together."

"OK!" JJ chimed in. "Let's bring attention to ALS and raise money for the new clinic I want to build here."

Raising $66,000 on Route 66 became the goal. In ten weeks, a caravan was assembled including thirteen Corvettes, two motor homes, and a film crew who came to capture the moments we visited with other PALS (people with ALS) en route to bring attention to this cruel disease. By the time we arrived five days later at the Santa Monica Pier in California, the group had raised $326,000 for the start of the clinic. This success was a result of how JJ did most things, exceeding expectations, always thinking about others, and making a difference in so many lives, with his kind and giving heart!

The second opinion confirmed an ALS diagnosis. And the disease ran its predictable course. During the last six months of JJ's life, the responsibility of feeding tubes, wheelchairs, and a talking device to communicate rested on my shoulders. Here is where I learned to stay in the present moment. I never allowed myself to think ahead to what my life would be like when this was over. I needed to respond to everyday changes so I could help us both live the life we chose together—in the present.

It was three days before Christmas, the tree lights were glowing, and all the ornaments were placed perfectly. The gifts were under the tree, and the grandchildren's toys were ready to be opened. JJ closed his eyes for the last time. It was just fifteen months from the time we heard, "It's ALS." JJ had always lived his life at warp speed, for sure! Did he live his life on earth with the faith and knowledge of where he was going from here? Yes!

This story may seem like it is about JJ more than about me. But that's not true. The ALS story was an event in both our lives, but I was the only one who survived the disease. I survived because, unlike JJ, I had a choice from the beginning. I chose to live the time I had with JJ fully, and doing this was the greatest gift of all. It was never about all the things we managed to do together. It was about loving life and not fearing death with a man who loved unconditionally, and accepted the same from me.

The outcome was yes, God did answer my prayer that day, with my shaking hands on the steering wheel, and JJ and I were never alone on our adventurous journey and beyond.

The ALS Center at Mercy Health St. Mary's Hospital in Grand Rapids, Michigan, opened nine months after JJ's death. Now serving over 400 families a year battling the same disease, it is helping them face the same trials we did, closer to their homes.

Events happen in life—it is the response to these events that give us outcomes. Choose the responses that come from love, and not fear. If we do so, I promise, as difficult as they may be, we will still succeed at this adventure that we all call life!

Pam Bouma Miller is the author of Undoing Conditional Love. Life Lessons in Love, Loss, and Forgiveness. She's a speaker and certified trainer in Jack Canfield methodology and Success Principles, helping those with challenges of uncertainty in life and business. Getting you from where you are, to where you want to be, living life fully and in the Present. Visit Pam's website at www.Pammillerconsulting.com or reach out to her at pam@pammillerconsulting.com.

My American Dream

By Dorota McKay

"Our life is what our thoughts make it."
— Marcus Aurelius

It was the fall of 2009, and I was living in a small cottage on the coast of Maine with my husband, Matt. It was a beautiful quiet spot on Saco Bay. I loved being able to take long walks on the beach, listen to the waves, breathe the salty ocean air, and watch how the surface of the ocean changed its hue depending on the weather conditions. Matt worked as a finance director for a non-profit camp and conference center and we were caretakers of the property during the off-season.

One night, Matt came home a lot less cheerful than usual. He had just lost his job, which also meant that we lost our housing and our only source of income. It was less than two years after we got married. I was still clinging to my old life by continuing doctoral studies in American Literature at the University of Maria Curie-Sklodowska in Lublin, Poland. I was a full-time student and I did not have a job, yet. The conference center where we stayed was quiet and empty at that time of year. All my friends were far away and I felt like I did not belong anywhere anymore. I was still a stranger in Maine, and my life in Poland seemed like a distant past. I felt completely helpless and unable to face the situation. As an English teacher with a Polish accent, I would have had a tough time finding employment while American schools and universities were laying off teachers by the thousands. The average job search took four to six months and millions of highly qualified US-born candidates were competing for lower-level positions. I remembered we were eating ramen noodles for dinner every night, trying to save money as we often had less than fifty dollars in our bank account.

As I walked down the deserted beach in Camp Ellis, looking at the ocean, the wind was blowing my hair around and tears were streaming down my face. I grew up in a communist country. We lived a modest life, but my parents worked very hard to make sure that we (the kids), never had to worry about what we were going to eat or where we were going to live. The possibility of not knowing how we were going to pay for food or shelter was new to me. The world had never seemed so unfriendly and threatening to me before. My vision became blurry as tears were filling up my eyes and I could hardly see where I was going. Suddenly, I tripped over a piece of driftwood sticking out of the sand and fell face forward into a small puddle. I choked on the sand and my hair and my clothes were completely drenched. My body felt exhausted and empty as if someone squeezed all the energy out of it.

In this state of total exhaustion and despair, my mind reached that point of emptiness and stillness, allowing me to focus on the present moment. Right in front of my eyes, there was a perfectly smooth piece of turquoise sea glass, its surface gleaming in the late afternoon sun. I was struck by the beauty of it and realized that had I not fallen down, I would have never found this little treasure. As I stared at it in awe, it reminded me of who I was. I was the resourceful little girl who delivered newspapers to make pocket money. I was that second-grader who earned a little bit of income by tutoring younger kids. I juggled three jobs in college so that I could support myself and travel the country with my boyfriend. As I thought of all this, I realized that I was not a victim and I had a choice of how I was going to respond to the situation. There was beauty and opportunity to be found in every obstacle and every hardship that I faced. I resolved to stop feeling sorry for myself. I was going to take matters into my own hands and find a way to provide for my family so that we could both thrive. I set the intention of achieving financial independence in the next five years, even though I had no idea as to how I was going to get there.

Once I assumed responsibility for my fate and resolved to change my situation, things started to happen. Ideas spontaneously came to mind. People suddenly showed up in my life and helped me come up with solutions. I decided to leave the doctoral program and change careers. I found a job as a waitress at a local restaurant and started taking night classes at a nearby community college. I made new friends and finally felt like I was a member of my local community.

I met a teacher who inspired me to become a CPA (certified public accountant). I took a tax internship and discovered that I was good at my new job. I joined a regional accounting and consulting firm and passed all my exams. Matt and I were able to buy a little starter home in Saco. I remember us peeling the old tobacco-stained wallpaper off the walls and painting them a crisp white color. It was one of the happiest times in my life.

We were able to invest and set aside a rainy-day fund. I then went on to work for a Big Four accounting firm in Boston and gained exposure to the world of publicly traded companies. From there, I moved on to a corporate career and our income has quadrupled in five years. I am now managing a department and I run my own teaching business on the side. Matt is still by my side and he is back to his usual cheerful self.

As I look over the past ten years, it all seems like a wonderful dream, even though things were not always easy. There were long nights at the restaurant, while I was mopping the floors and wondering whatever came of my graduate degree and my plan of becoming an English professor. There were days when I had no time to eat all day while I was working towards multiple deadlines. I remember falling asleep on the floor next to my desk as I was studying for my professional exams late into the night. All those difficulties contributed to who I am today and transformed me as a person. I have become comfortable with uncertainty, and I approach life with curiosity and excitement. I am ready to take the next step in my personal development journey, knowing that I have control over my outcomes. I can be successful by adjusting my response to any given situation, regardless of what happens in my life.

I weathered the storm and I want to help you do the same. If you are currently struggling, life seems hard and you have no idea how things could change for the better, remember my story. Know that everything that happens to you is somehow for your benefit. Pause and look around you and discover how much you already have to be grateful for. Know that things can improve for you very quickly once you set an intention to take charge of your life and apply yourself towards your goals with faith and gratitude. The American dream that allows anyone, regardless of where they were born or what class they were born into, to attain their own version of success is still alive and well.

Dorota McKay is a creative problem solver with a passion for finance and personal development. As the founder of BeaconCliff, she helps finance teams achieve high performance through her transformational workshops and process improvement events that combine the Success Principles with elements of Six Sigma, Kaizen, and other management tools and philosophies. She is also a corporate finance executive and holds active CPA, CMA, CFE, and CTT Practitioner designations. For additional information on Finance Transformation events and tools visit www.beaconcliff.com.

Heidi and Andrea:
A Love Story

By Philip Daunt

"The lives we live are the result of the choices we make."
— Anonymous

I choose to believe that I am responsible for the choices I make and the consequences of those choices, both intended and unintended. Living this belief has transformed my life.

In February 1985, I said yes to an invitation that I had received from a friend, Sharon, to go on a blind date with someone named Heidi. I had no idea that saying yes to Sharon's invitation would change my life forever. On the appointed day, Heidi showed up at my office. I was a thirty-three-year-old lawyer in a three-piece pinstripe suit, practicing with a small law firm in Monterey, California. I had moved from Detroit, Michigan to the Monterey Peninsula a few months before. Heidi was a twenty-two-year-old student at MIIS (the Monterey Institute of

International Studies), dressed in a white tee-shirt and a blue jean skirt. What we had in common was our ability to speak French. I had lived in Brussels for three years between undergraduate school and law school. Heidi had been an AFS (American Field Service) student in high school in Lyon and had taken classes at the Sorbonne in Paris.

Early in our relationship, Heidi told me something that struck me: "Philip, I believe that the lives we live are the results of the choices we make." I chose to try on that belief, and I have stuck with it ever since.

Years later, I learned a formula that helped me to experience more deeply the meaning of that statement: $E+R=O$. The Events in our lives plus our Responses to those Events produce the Outcomes we experience in our lives. We often do not have control over the Events in our lives, but we do have control over how we choose to Respond to those Events. And by changing our Responses, we can change our Outcomes and transform our lives.

A few months after I met Heidi, she graduated from MIIS, and she left for a summer job in Europe, guiding a group of teenagers from Rome to Paris on bicycles. I arranged to meet her in Europe after she had completed her summer job. I wanted Heidi to meet my parents, and I also wanted her to meet my grandmother. The time with my parents went great. They got along really well. However, it was when I saw how kind and gentle Heidi was with my grandmother, that I knew I had finally found the woman I wanted to marry. The trouble was in convincing Heidi that marrying me was a good idea for Heidi.

Recommitting to my belief that the lives we live are the results of the choices we make, I visualized being married to Heidi. I chose to pursue my goal of marrying her with a quiet persistence. I did not give up. Finally, in February 1987, Heidi said yes, and in May 1988, we tied the knot. My goal was achieved. My blind date had turned into my life partner, the most beautiful woman I had ever known, both inside and out!

Fast forward to the Fall of 1992. I was a forty-one-year-old lawyer. I had a successful law practice. I was married to Heidi, still the most beautiful woman I had ever known. We were living in our own home in a nice, quiet neighborhood near the top of the hill. Our son, Trevor, was a happy, healthy, and precocious little boy. All that was missing to complete our family was a little sister for Trevor.

Andrea Katherine was born on November 22, 1992, a few days after Trevor's third birthday. As expected, she was beautiful! Of course, she was! She was Heidi's daughter! I thought that my life was complete.

Then things began to unravel.

Days after Andrea was born, we were referred to a pediatric neurologist, who told us that our baby had a recessive genetic defect called Spinal Muscular Atrophy or SMA. He said it was always fatal. He would be surprised if Andrea lived to be a year old.

We took Andrea to UCSF in San Francisco for a second opinion. There, the chairman of the Pediatric Neurology Department confirmed the local neurologist's diagnosis: Andrea had SMA.

It turns out that Heidi and I are both SMA carriers. Both parents have to be carriers in order for a child to have SMA. However, when both parents are carriers, there is a one-in-four chance that any child born to those parents will have the disease. Trevor had dodged the genetic bullet; he was a carrier of the disease, but he was healthy, just like his parents.

On March 15, 1993, Andrea died in our arms in Kona, Hawaii. It was the day after my 42nd birthday. She was three months and twenty-one days old. We brought her ashes back to Monterey, and I experienced my life shift.

For the last twenty-seven years, I have chosen to look to Andrea for emotional and spiritual guidance as I go through my daily life. Andrea has taught me not to take anything for granted in my life. Because Heidi and I were healthy, I had assumed that our baby would be healthy. I had also assumed that I had control over the important events in my life. Andrea taught me that both assumptions were not true.

Trying to make sense of something that didn't make any sense to me led me to question the beliefs that I had. I learned to embrace the paradox of surrendering to and accepting the events in my life and at the same time taking complete responsibility for my responses to those events.

Questioning my role as a litigator, I chose to explore alternative ways of engaging in and resolving conflicts. I chose to train as a mediator. I chose to explore various methods and modalities of personal growth, looking for ways to change my life for the better.

Years of working on myself have transformed my life. Today, I am not a typical lawyer, and I am not a typical mediator. In both of my practices, I help my clients to transform their legal problems into opportunities for personal growth and positive change. I do this by helping my clients to give up self-pity, anger and resentment, and the need to be right and make other people wrong, and instead to look for solutions that work for everyone.

Today, Heidi is still the most beautiful woman I have ever known, and we are still happily married. Many marriages fail after the death of a child. Our marriage is stronger than it has ever been. With every setback, disappointment, and heartache, we have chosen to recommit to our marriage and to each other. We have chosen to look for solutions that work for both of us, acknowledging that we sometimes choose to have different opinions, and we sometimes choose to have different ways of responding to the events, problems, and heartaches that arise in our lives. We both choose to believe that different is not wrong. We both believe that our commitment to our marriage and to each other is far more important than any differences of opinion or different ways of responding to the events that arise in our lives.

After Andrea died, Heidi and I chose to have another child, knowing that there was a one-in-four chance that this child would have the same disease that had taken Andrea from us. Andrea's younger sister, Alora, like her brother and her parents, is an SMA carrier, but she is a healthy, beautiful, intelligent, loving, and courageous woman, much like her mother. I cannot imagine living in a world without her. I am so grateful for her presence in my life!

I believe that who I am today and the life that I live today are the results of the choices I have made in my life, including choosing to say yes to a blind date over thirty years ago and choosing to take responsibility for how I responded to the death of a baby girl who died over twenty-seven years ago.

By choosing to believe that the lives we live are the results of the choices we make, rather than believing that our lives are the results of events beyond our control, we can take control over our destiny, we can actively engage in the transformation of our lives. By giving up anger, resentment, shame, self-pity, and the need to be right and make other people wrong, we transform our lives for the better. The events in our lives plus our responses to those events produce the outcomes we experience in our lives. By changing our responses to the events in our lives, we can change our outcomes and we can transform our lives.

Philip Daunt has been an attorney for almost forty years and a mediator for over twenty-five. As a transformational lawyer, he helps his clients to transform their legal problems into opportunities for personal growth and positive change. He considers himself to be a professional conflict manager and a conscious conflict engagement coach. He thinks of conflict as a state of being that results from having unmet expectations. He believes that the ultimate answer to every problem and to every heartache is love, compassion, empathy, kindness, and gratitude for everyone and for everything. He may be reached at philip@philipdaunt.com.

THE GREATEST GIFT OF ALL

By Louise Neel Hoeyer

"The two most important days in your life is the day you are born,
and the day you find out why."
— Mark Twain

It was the summer of 2011. Outside, the sun shined bright from a blue sky. At Islands Brygge, one of the upcoming areas in Copenhagen, the capital of Denmark, families and friends were strolling down the boardwalk. The harbor entrance was full of people in kayaks and small motorboats enjoying themselves on this sunny August day.

My husband and I lived here in one of the newly built apartment houses, together with our two boys, Arthur, a toddler at two, and Vitus, the proud big brother, at the age of five. We had moved to Islands Brygge some years before, as soon as the apartment was ready, and loved being part of this new urban and flourishing neighborhood.

We were in our late thirties and we both had interesting careers, great friends, and well-functional families.

For many years I had worked in the IT industry. In later years I worked as a manager within internal communications, being an important advisor for management in the companies I worked in. My friends described me as ambitious, dedicated, and hardworking. And that was definitely me. If there was something I needed to understand or a new skill I needed to learn I just put extra time and effort into the subject until I could apply it. Hard work and long hours always got me the results I wanted.

When Vitus was born, I was already a manager and I kept working full-time because, in my mind, a manager could not work part-time. I felt acknowledged in my role as a manager. Further, it was a well-paid job. I was involved in many exciting projects and I often got admiring glances, when I told others what I did for a living.

Like any other first-time family, my husband and I had to juggle our many roles; as a couple, as parents, as part of our family, and in our roles at work. For me, that meant using all my waking hours trying to be a great mother, a dedicated and loyal people manager, a loving wife and compassionate friend, and a caring daughter and sister. Sleep was short and often interrupted by crying kids.

One day, I was in our kitchen making myself a cup of coffee. From there I could see my husband and our two boys playing. They were doing a puzzle together and they were all enjoying the moment.

Looking at them, I suddenly realized that I did not feel anything towards them. I could not feel any joy, any gratitude, or any love. It was like I was cut off from my neck down. I searched for positive feelings and I found nothing. Only emptiness and numbness.

My stomach knotted. What was happening? I was a successful woman in my late thirties, married to a loving, caring, and good-looking man who had given me two wonderful boys. We had many friends and our families were healthy. I lived in a fancy part of Copenhagen. We both had good incomes and were able to do almost everything we wanted. What was wrong with me?

This was not how my life was supposed to be. I had to do something. But what should I do?

As many times before in my life, I didn't involve anyone in what I had just experienced. I felt too ashamed and embarrassed. So I started to search for answers on my own.

For what felt like a long time, nothing changed. But then one day I came across a woman I had met when I was taking my Master's at the University of Aarhus. Some years ago, she had finalized a Master's degree and a Ph.D. in children's learning patterns and digital communication, but now she worked as a scientific hand analyst and intuitive counselor, helping people identifying their life purpose – their unique gift. Somehow, that resonated with me and I felt a spark of hope. Maybe she could help me. Without really knowing why or what to expect, I booked a session with her.

I had my session with her in her house late that September. She shared with me so many things about me that nobody knew and together we uncovered my life purpose. It felt like coming home. I felt seen, heard, and understood at my core. This was me!

The session blew me away and I wanted more. One session became many and, little by little, I tried to implement some of the suggestions she gave me in my life. I started to walk in nature and to take online courses about self-care and self-development.

At first, I felt guilty. Guilty about taking time on my own. I felt that I was letting go of my responsibility as a mother. But the healing of nature had a profound impact on me. It was like a big wave I could not stop.

Diving deeper into my life purpose, I understood that I spent a lot of my time on the wrong things. In so many years I had tried to do what I thought others wanted from me and I had abandoned myself in my quest to be accepted.

Slowly, I started to align what I spent my time on at work and at home to my life purpose. I let go of my manager position to free up time so I could join interesting networks, take more self-development courses, and complete a special education I had wanted for a long time. The more I used my life purpose as the guiding principle for my choices, the lighter things became, I got more energy and I started to feel joyful again.

One day, a friend recommended a book called *The Success Principles* by Jack Canfield. I was taken aback. Not only did the principles resonate deeply within me, but one of the principles, Be Clear Why You Are Here, was about the importance of finding your life purpose.

Since then, I have used Jack Canfield's methods and meditations to explore my life purpose further and I continue to add layers to my special gift: inspiring and empowering others to use their unique talents and create a meaningful life on purpose, by sharing what I learn and experience on my life journey.

Finding my life purpose and living my life on purpose has been life-changing for me. It has truly transformed the way I see and live my life. I have been able to create a life and a career I love, because I have found my magic spark – the flowing energy that makes it easy for me to live, love, and laugh from the bottom of my heart every day, and that is, for me, the greatest gift of all.

Louise is a partner at HUMAN UNIVERZ, where she works as a change manager, trainer, speaker, and mentor. She has over seventeen years of experience moving people and businesses effectively from where they are to where they want to be by using approaches, methods, and tools from the disciplines of change management, change communication, behavioral design, personal development, human psychology, neuroscience, and mindset. Louise holds a Master in Media Studies and Sociology and has taken numerous training sessions and courses on leadership and communication. She is certified in Prosci® ADKAR®, Actee, Behavioral Design, The Success Principles, and The Canfield Methodology. Louise can be reached by email: louiseh@humanuniverz.com or via LinkedIn at https://www.linkedin.com/in/louise-neel-hoeyer/.

THE SEED WITHIN

By Rupali Trehan

"For a star to be born, there is one thing that must happen: a gaseous nebula must collapse. So collapse. Crumble. This is not your destruction. This is your birth."
— Zoe Skylar

"**M**om!" my four-year-old son called in his ever-enthusiastic voice. "I just fell down. Yay!" Nudging the left side of his chest with his tiny fist, he added, "I just told my heart, hey buddy you've become stronger. It is good to fall. Let's go."

Flashback thirty years or so, when I was a child, (an intelligent one, or so I would like to believe), a fall was something to be afraid of. I vividly recall, each time I fell, I was asked to hit/attack the source of the fall in an attempt to overpower it. To a background score of "How dare that thing make you fall," I was made to believe that falling/failing meant becoming weak. This belief I carried with me into my twenties. Till then I had experienced my so-called share of falling/

failing—like the time I lost my boyfriend to my best friend. Or when my boss criticized and fired me from my first job (I call it feedback now); or when Oscar, my pet dog of thirteen years, passed away. True to my core, in response to each fall, I turned outward and blamed the source/reason for my fall. All in all, life was good.

It was only on October 1st, 2003 that I encountered my first life-changing fall. Eagerly awaiting my father's visit to start his study program alongside mine, I got a phone call. My father had passed away in a sudden car crash on his way to the airport, to board his flight to my city. I remember feeling a sudden whirlwind of emotions within me. The phone call made no sense to me. And nor did my life, thereafter.

I was twenty-three and I had fallen big. Emotionally. Mentally. Physically. My only response to this life-changing event was to attack the source. I looked outward and blamed God for everything. I played the role of a victim to perfection and as an award, graduated with the lowest GPA (Grade Point Average) in my MBA (Master of Business Administration) program. A big win for the victim in me! For the first time, life was not so good.

Fast forward sixteen years, and I hear the words: *event, response,* and *outcome.* Only this time, they were spoken by my mentor, Jack Canfield, amidst a room full of love and inspiration. I had signed up for a *Train the Trainer* program in the United States and it was here that I was exposed to his fundamental success principle: *E (event) + R (response) = O (outcome).*

I paused for a while. Then, I breathed in the principle, and I breathed out a huge sigh of relief. I experienced my first real epiphany. My life flashed before me, and I realized that up until now, the story I had been telling myself regarding the undesirable events in my life, had taken my power away. I responded to every fall/failure with an outward search that resulted in attacking/blaming the external source. But by making the outcome dependent on my ability to respond, I suddenly became all-powerful again. I felt high. Not the intoxicating type. But the one that lasts a lifetime. The revelation did not just stop there. I learned that in life we do anything and everything for a feeling that we derive from that experience. So while my father could not physically return to my world, the feeling that I felt when with him could. I could feel unconditional love again! I could receive guidance from a loved one, again! I could spend time with someone without being judged at all, again! In retrospect, every event and every experience in my life slowly started to make sense. I felt the same high again. Not the intoxicating type. But the one that lasts a lifetime.

I could feel my second real epiphany on the way. Falling/Failing is painful. Most often, it will change the landscape of our relationships, finances, and mental wellbeing. But, underneath the pain lies the most novel and valuable seeds to growth and success. But to find those seeds, one must turn inward and not outward. And nurturing those seeds with resilience and perseverance will ensure the desired fruit of success. So how, then, does falling/failing weaken you? In fact, by opening your mind-set and strengthening your heart-set, it aids you in your journey to success.

In the trainer program, one of the instructors introduced six words that had a lasting impact on my intellect: "Is this story really serving me?" With a curious mind and a brave heart, I started to question some of the stories/beliefs I had been telling myself. My belief (falling/failing in life weakens you) was immediately put to the test. Every time I failed at something, circumstances around me changed. This change made me uncomfortable. To resist being uncomfortable, I gave birth to fear. And choosing to give full power to this fear, I slipped into victim mode. I now began to question the validity of this belief. If only I chose to keep fear as a silent spectator, and instead of resisting the unknown, or the uncomfortable, or the unfamiliar, I embrace it like an opportunity—an opportunity that could be a source of growth.

So what, then, does it mean to fall/fail? Is it not that each fall reveals valuable insights about who we are? Was it not the loss of my loved one that implanted the seed of compassion in me? How would I value loyalty in relationships if disloyalty had never shown up? In other words, it is not falling/failing but the self-created fear of falling/failing that stops us from finding those seeds!

Sharing the same enthusiasm as my four-year-old, I urge you to fall. Fall big. Find the seeds within. And with perseverance plant those seeds; only to see the magic happen. The rise! The mighty rise!

Rupali Trehan loves creating joy. As a certified coach, she finds the term mental health depressing to begin with. Everyone is a work in progress and possibilities lie everywhere. The journey to discovering them is fun, fierce, and phenomenal. My Daily Cup of Joy, her entrepreneurial venture, is enabling her to customize special one-to-one programs for her clients – now friends. At home (New Delhi, India) she holds her family children closest to her heart and celebrates all their stories. She can be contacted at rupalitrehan@omyaainc.com

TAKE 100% RESPONSIBILITY

No Blaming, No Complaining, No Excuse Making

Change your response until you achieve your desired outcome.

BEING WILLING TO PAY THE PRICE

By Mark Hugh Sam

"A man is but a product of his thoughts.
What he thinks, he becomes."
— Mahatma Gandhi

As I was riding the Maokong Gondola alone in the dark to see the nightlights of Taipei, I heard the ping from my mobile. It was days before Christmas 2018, and I was now single again. Just a month earlier, in November, I returned custody of my three youngest children to their mother after reversing an August 2018 hard-won custody decision in my favor. In early December, I had a major disagreement with my best friend. The one constant in all three events was me: I sucked at relationships.

What made these events sting more was that I had already tried to give myself a make-over. For what I had called Mark 2.0, I had made relationships the most important thing in my life. By the time I had reached the top of Maokong, I had made a decision that I was going to do whatever it took to change and enable myself to achieve both wealth and love—and most importantly, to sustain them. In my self-development journey, I had read that your exterior world is a reflection of your interior world. It was obvious that my interior world, my mind, needed changing. I decided that Mark 3.0 was going to have a beautiful interior world.

I had recently read Dr. Carol Dweck's work about mindsets and realized that my habitual orientation to life was with a type of fixed mindset (wanting to look smart) rather than with a growth mindset. Although one can change one's mindset, I had done nothing to change mine. Now I was motivated to change, particularly as I realized how my fixed mindset had limited me throughout my life.

The growth mindset involves believing you can learn and improve in anything – through effort. I had lived virtually my entire life with a false growth mindset, which involves believing that one is devoted to learning and becoming a better person, but actually is avoiding challenges, giving up easily, ignoring useful feedback—hence, a fixed mindset. Like most limited beliefs, my false growth (and actually fixed) mindset was formed when I was a child.

When I was young, I was indeed smart. At the same time, I had low self-esteem, probably because when I was a toddler I didn't speak until I was almost four years old. I was tested for all kinds of things and the doctors reassured my parents that I was not dumb (literally meaning not able to talk) nor was I stupid. However, after hearing this for two years and having people concerned about me, I am sure my toddler-brain picked up that maybe I was indeed not so smart, or literally dumb.

When I did start talking, I would not stop talking. My favorite word was "Why?" Adults would try to shut me up, disparaging my "plastic mouth." This was also not good for a very curious child who had just found his voice.

I was fortunate to be very good at math and also to have learned how to use wooden blocks to count and add with great accuracy. I would play with them continuously. I was also fortunate that, even though I was a poor reader in the beginning, Ms. Wong, an after-school teacher, helped me to become an above-average reader and really gave me the love of reading, which has been the foundation for my love of learning and inborn curiosity.

So I was able to develop an identity of being smart, but I still had low self-esteem. So. in order to hold onto my identity as being smart, I would do things to ensure that I looked smart—and this became a trap for me—I was an avid learner, but I was learning because I liked being regarded as smart. In fact, however, I was playing it safe. Knowing stuff came naturally got me all kinds of kudos, but I had not learned to work hard to achieve the desired result.

A Turning Point with a Dedicated "Turn"

Let's flashback to the beginning of the story, where receiving bad news in three core areas of my life had brought me to my knees. From there, I knew I had to change—not just by reading another book or learning a new self-motivational technique. I realized that to create a new future, I needed to rewire my brain!

My first glimmer that this was even possible occurred when I happened upon the website www.mindsetworks.com. There, I found a simple eight-question mindset test. The results, and the follow-up exploration I did to understand them, gave a new lens that brought my life, with all its impressive successes and equally spectacular crashes, into breathtakingly sharp focus. I realized that I had been operating from a strongly fixed mindset—one that took me to early plateaus, but never grew my potential. I avoided feedback. I saw strong effort as fruitless (or a sign that one was stupid), and I gave up easily. In a few words, I had made a lifelong habit of looking good but actually playing small. Very small, and with excruciatingly painful results for myself, and those I loved.

But then I discovered the good news: mindset can be changed! Did I dare believe this? I was no stranger to assertions about how to change oneself. I had tried out many of them, sporadically, and with, not surprisingly, spotty results. But this claim was different—more modest and common sense, perhaps, but more believable. For me, the key to being open to learning about mindset was reading about the double-blind research study Carol Dweck undertook to determine whether a fixed mindset could be changed. She gave a course on growth mindset to Class A, to Class B she gave a normal study habits course, and nothing to Class C. She did this several times, and for several thousand students. She compared their results to another learning task. Class A, who had been taught how to have a growth mindset, had significantly outperformed Class B and Class C.

Dweck taught the students in Class A two key facts: 1) that brain neurology actually changes when you make an effort in response to a challenge, and 2) the only way neurons grow in the brain and make new pathways is when an effort is made. Therefore, the brain is not fixed in terms of a given amount of talent or intelligence! We can actually grow new neurons and connections in any area of the brain. For example, we may start out with a certain amount of neural connections related to making art, but we can grow new neurons at any age as we practice art. Therefore, we are not born with limited abilities. We are born with a brain that can grow our abilities in whatever area we desire.

Results of my Personal Mindset Experiment

Convinced by Dweck's results, I saw mindset as the root cause of my recurrent life-success-and-subsequent-failure cycle. Clearly, I could learn but needed to learn to value my own effort more than my own native intelligence. I needed to foster my own persistence and engagement when the going got tough, rather than abandoning the effort because it had gotten too hard. I needed to form new habits of seeking feedback, and trusting others' intelligence, rather than plowing ahead on the basis of my own perspectives and estimations.

I decided to do whatever it took to rework my mindset. How did I do that? Essentially, I gave myself the course that Dr. Dweck gave her students in the mindset group. I learned all I could about how the brain responds to effort, and how effort results in learning. I learned to tolerate setbacks as part of the learning process. I caught myself in the act of wanting to quit and instead, persisted. I sought out challenges that were hard for me (and in the process, learned to accept that many things were hard!), and set my goal as learning something valuable rather than appearing to others as successful.

After months of work, I retook the test. It confirmed, after only four months of dedicated effort, that I now had a growth mindset. My results, and those of many others, show that you can indeed change your mindset and continue to develop throughout your life. I now believe I can improve in anything! Now, I have improved my abilities – I can take the risk, I am resilient, I can take feedback, I can set goals.

Once I was able to dramatically improve my growth mindset, I set out to change my core beliefs, habits of thoughts, personal identity, and character traits. During the process, I created what I call my loving inner world—and this includes a loving stance toward my own efforts and the growth they lead me to. I have also taken steps to become an entrepreneur, which is a huge step from being an advisor (my previous *low stakes* career), and one that requires me to hone my growth mindset every day. I am in the process of changing my exterior world, now that I have changed my interior world. The best is yet to come!

If my story has you suspecting that there are parts of you that have a fixed mindset, I challenge you to take stock of what it might be costing you. But don't stop there! Change to a growth mindset in as many ways as you can, and in as many areas of your life as you can. It will take persistent effort, but this is a fair price for what you will save in pain, time, and unfruitful pursuits that might look good but are not borne from your own soulful desires. Determine that you are about growth through effort and you will find yourself becoming the best and most highly engaged person you can be.

Mark Hugh Sam is an entrepreneur, trainer, and father of six children. After living a roller-coaster life, he was able to create his loving inner world. Now, his mission is to use knowledge and skill to be an exemplar and to help others to be their best selves as we create a better world together. His 2040 goal is to create ten+ businesses, mentor or invest in 2,000+ entrepreneurs, and teach ten+ million people. Mark Hugh Sam is a Chinese, Jamaican, Canadian living in Indonesia. You can reach him at www.markhughsam.com.

Ask, Listen: You Will Change Your Opinion

By Aparna Vemuri

"If you wish to see the truth, then hold no opinion for or against."
— Frequently attributed to Rajneesh, or Sengcan

"You didn't do it right, anna (brother), you didn't do it right."
I was crying, my hands banging on my brother's hospital bed. How can he do this without giving us time to prepare for his loss? Even the doctors said his condition was not critical, but he only needed medical attention. They gave me permission to go home to bring him something to eat. Within the hour we received a call from the hospital, and I rushed back only to see the doctors trying to revive him from a cardiac arrest.

My brother, who was fifty-four, strong and positive, was hoping to come back with much more energy and fulfill his responsibilities, succumbed to death unexpectedly. He had been ill with diabetes and was on dialysis three times a week, but we never thought he was so ill that it was life-threatening.

My father died when my brother was sixteen. After completing his degree in chemical engineering, my brother took over the family responsibilities from my sister, saw three of his sisters married, and only then thought about doing anything for himself. Later, he also married, happily taking care of his family and our mom.

My brother was a very dynamic, arrogant, and sarcastic person. That's how I saw him since childhood because we used to fight a lot. We carried our childhood rivalry into adulthood. Continuing the rivalry did not mean that we fought as we did as kids, but we had our own boundaries drawn and we never opened up to discuss anything from our hearts. However, we both respected each other and were deeply concerned about the wellbeing of each other.

All of this changed in June 2019, when my brother was hospitalized with multiple fractures in his right leg due to a fall in the bathroom. I went to see him, and we both had tears to see each other. For the first time, he lovingly held my hand in his and asked if I would stay there and visit him daily during the entire stay in hospital.

"Of course," I said, without any hesitation.

Every day I visited him and stayed there for three to four hours. We discussed global, political, and general topics. Simply conversing with each other went a long way in diminishing the communication barrier set up between us. At that moment, I went a step deeper into our relationship and asked about his life and how he was doing.

In 2006, he was involved in a transaction with someone without knowing that person was under departmental surveillance. This association falsely tarnished my brother's reputation. I wasn't aware of these false allegations. I asked him to share what exactly had happened. I was surprised to see his courage as he narrated what had happened a decade ago. I often wonder where, and how, I found the courage to ask him.

When I heard his complete story around the allegations and the false case filed against him, tears filled my eyes. These were tears of empathy for the emotional pain he might have gone through and tears of joy for cleansing my negative impression of him.

During our conversation, I noticed something that really struck me. So, I asked him about his spiritual evolution. I'd always known of his strict two-to-three hours in a meditative state to chant and perform daily rituals. I was awestruck when he mentioned how he made a "deal with the Divine," to help him shed his ego.

Shivratri is the day when there is a natural upsurge of spiritual energies in human beings. Between 2007 and 2009, on every Shivratri, he completely immersed himself into a higher awakening state and submerged himself in bliss. During those ecstatic moments, he committed to shedding his ego that stemmed out of authority, power, and self-centered acts.

The first blow was to his career, due to the false allegation. But he did not pay much attention to it because he knew he was clean. He did not care about the change in his own environment, which came from his immediate family and relatives. It made him aware, though, that his self-esteem had hit rock bottom. That is when he asked the Divine to intervene, to help him out of this fall. He decided and promised to compromise any other area of his life to save his career, and would never ask for anything thereon. And in just a couple of months, everything was resolved.

Following that clearance came the second blow to his health. Since 2011, his health had been slowly deteriorating. But he kept his word. Whatever he went through, he never asked for help or intervention from the Divine, such was his determination to keep his word to God.

I am here, on October 14, making arrangements for the final rites of my loving brother. I would have never known about all this had I not spent time with him, talking. Had I not listened to him and his side of the story, I would not have changed my opinion of him.

Now, I have tears of joy, not of repentance, and carry sweet memories of him.

Aparna Vemuri is a spiritual alchemist and intuitive healer. She helps people to improve their relationship with themselves and others. She can be reached at www.aparnavemuri.com.

Don't Stand Still: You Could Get Run Over!

By Stuart B. Fields

"Just remember, you can do anything you set your mind to, but it takes action, perseverance and facing your fears."
— Gillian Anderson

We were thirteen years old. My best friend Jeff and I were adventurous and avid bicyclists. We traveled everywhere by bicycle. Jeff's dad was an amateur rock-hound and owned the Rock Shop of Appleton. When Jeff found an article in his dad's shop about gold discoveries in a Wisconsin lake, we both got gold fever. Our summer adventure was about to begin! We were going for the gold with dreams of getting rich.

Nugget Lake was on the other side of the state. But at age thirteen, all we had for our transportation that summer was our bicycles. So, we loaded up our bikes, borrowed round pie tins from my mom for panning, and took off, filled with dreams of striking it rich. It can't be said for sure, but I think we might even have had a sign on our bikes proclaiming, "Gold or Bust!" It was an adventure, and we were elated with a sense of possibility.

Fully loaded with gear, professional touring bikes can weigh upwards of seventy pounds. As teens, we could not afford professional. Our older bikes and homemade camping equipment weighed much more. We had luggage and camping equipment hanging off both sides of the bike. We had packs on the front and packs on the back, with additional gear on top of rear racks. But we were fueled with determination.

You might be asking why parents would let thirteen-year-old boys adventure across the state alone by bicycle – but it was the early seventies. Jeff and I were middle children in larger families (Jeff had four siblings, I had six). Our parents had already experienced the challenges of our older siblings' adventures and tenacity to follow through. So, they didn't argue. They simply wished us luck and thought we would be back soon, smiling knowingly about our foolish adventure.

In 1973, kids did not have cell phones. The internet did not exist. GPS systems had just been launched by the US government. Certainly, this technology was not available to a couple of thirteen-year-old junior high school kids like us. Instead, we navigated using paper maps. County maps gave us the most detail, but none indicated bike trails. We relied on following back roads, county trunk roads, and on the rare occasion, a busier highway. Mostly we were interested in the most direct but least traveled route that would take us to Nugget Lake.

We managed to cross the state in six days; averaging between fifty and seventy miles per day. It was only when we got close to our destination that we discovered our navigational error. The highway bridge we had expected – and which was indicated on the map – turned out to be a railroad bridge.

The bridge was 150 feet across, spanning the Chippewa River where the rapids were visible seventy-five feet below the trestle. The rails were shiny, which should have been a warning sign to us, but we were not that clever.

This was a decision point. Either we could risk crossing the railroad trestle over the river, or detour to one of the busy highways and cross on a highway bridge.

The incentive to cross the railroad bridge increased when we investigated our options. To reach either of the highway bridges that spanned the river would require a lot of biking. According to the map, there were two highway bridges. One was located to the north and one to the south. We calculated the distance to be twenty-five miles to the north or twenty-five miles to the south, so both bridge alternatives were equidistant from us. Our destination was immediately on the other side of the river. But twenty-five miles of biking either way also meant twenty-five miles back, adding fifty miles to our trip.

Since we were averaging fifty miles a day, the cost to us would be a full day of biking. An additional day of travel delayed our arrival at the destination. Each day cost us more of our precious savings in food and fees for camping sites. We were tired as we pondered our options, and it was already late in the afternoon. In the end, we opted not to stretch out our trip by another day and started to walk our bikes across the bridge.

There were no railings, no walkways, no support, and nowhere to hide if a train came. Jeff and I pushed cautiously, one railroad tie after the other, with our heavy bikes undulating up and down like horses as we rolled towards the distant goal. One step, one push; when the bike front tire rose, the back tire dropped into the space between the railroad ties. Then the front tire dipped, and the back tire rose as we passed the next set of railroad ties. Gently, cautiously pushing our bikes, we moved forward like caterpillars on a tree branch. Scared, yes! However, we thought the shortcut was worth the risk. We would be saving an entire day of biking—and it was late. Our destination was on the other side and it also looked like a good camping area for the night.

We were about seventy-five feet across the bridge, with fifty feet to go, when Jeff asked, "Stuart, what would you do if a train came?"

"I dunno," I said. "Maybe run, maybe jump."

Jeff had no sooner uttered these words when around the bend, directly in front of us, a freight train came barreling towards us – lights on, horn blaring. We froze. We had traversed too far to safely return to our starting point. The only alternative was to continue forward. We had to run toward the oncoming train that did not see us, two small figures in the middle of a bridge, where we were most certainly not meant to be.

Fueled by adrenaline and fear, hoisting our gear-filled bikes up to our shoulders, we leaned forward and sprinted towards the train as it continued to rush towards us. It was then that Jeff dropped his tire pump! It had been attached to his frame. He knelt to pick it up.

"Jeff, just leave it. RUN!" I shouted over my shoulder. That was the last image I held of my friend. The train was getting closer, I feared for my life and feared even more for losing my friend who had dropped behind me. How would I explain his death to his parents and mine? I certainly did not want to bike home alone, grieving my friend—how could I? I barely reached the far shore when I tossed my bike to the left of the train tracks onto the gravel bank that was built up at the head of the bridge. Once my bike was clear I dove on the top of it and skidded to a stop – bruised and cut, but not too badly. I was safe for the moment.

But what about Jeff?

When I dove out of the way of the onrushing train, I tumbled about ten feet down the bank. The train roared by, and I felt the wind in its wake. Stunned, bruised, and winded from the fall, I struggled to catch my breath. Then came the moment of dread. I slowly crawled up the steep bank to the top of the rails to see what had happened to my friend. To my amazement, his head popped up on the opposite side of the rails. As it turned out, he dove to the right, as I was flying to the left of the oncoming train, having the same fears for my life that I had had for his. We rejoiced at being alive and seeing that the other had lived too!

We never did find gold. Instead, the experience was so traumatic that we decided to pedal south to the highway bridge the next day and begin our return journey home. I often reflect on that experience, many years later. I know there is a movie titled *Stand By Me*, which comes very close to the truth of capturing what we experienced. I think that there were many lessons to apply to our experience.

Taking action is the best principle that captures our story. From the beginning of our initial planning, we started taking action. We had a target in mind, but we had to prepare our bikes for the twelve-day trip. We took action to get ready. Then, we got moving and we navigated closer to our goal each day, one crank of the pedal after the other, growing muscles and our sense of pride with each passing mile. Then, we took crucial action to save ourselves when it became clear that our plan had taken a dramatic turn for the worse and required decisive alteration.

Life's experience has taught me that one must take action to get ahead. Sometimes, one must take action to survive! Without action, I would not be here to tell this story. Ironically, the action that saved our lives was facing the fear of an oncoming train. *Leaning into it* (or rather, hurtling ourselves past it), we ran toward danger knowing it was our only way out. And because we did not hesitate, we lived to have many more adventures.

Stuart Fields is a global workshop leader, speaker, transformational trainer, and coach. Having worked in the USA, Japan, England, and Poland, Stu is a certified Canfield Success Principles trainer who uplifts adult learners around the world. During the pandemic of 2020, Stu virtually brought together twenty-one human potential experts/authors and interviewed them with his signature compassionate style to launch the Unleash the Leader Within virtual summit. This summit was a beacon of light during dark times, highlighting the individual power each person has to overcome tremendous challenges on their path to success. www.stuartbfields.com.

Face What Isn't Working

By Susan Brown

"Growth is painful. Change is painful. But nothing is as painful as
staying stuck somewhere you don't belong."
— Mandy Hale

November 2, 1979, is a night that I will never forget. A night
that my life changed course. I was a new mom, my daughter
Jennifer was about six weeks old. My husband, Mike, and I had been
married for about a year and a half. I had been spending lots of time
inside the house adjusting to being a new mom. I was beginning to
recognize that my marriage was not what I hoped it would be once
we had started a family. I was feeling lost and was struggling to figure
out what to do. That night, I put Jennifer to bed and decided that I
would take a much-needed walk. Jennifer was fed and sleeping, and
Mike could watch her. It was a crisp, clear, and cold November night.
The moon was full and the sky was lit with stars. I was walking, taking
my time, thinking about my situation, and wondering what to do. As

I was heading back towards the house I happened to look up and saw a shooting star in the dark sky. I wondered if it meant something.

As I walked into the house the telephone was ringing. It was my father. "There's been an accident."

My heart stopped. "Are you okay?"

"It's your brother and a girl," he said. "They were in a car accident and are being transported to the hospital by ambulance." My dad asked if he and my mom could stay with us after they had been to the hospital to see my brother, Arnie. They lived on a farm about forty-five minutes outside of the city.

"Of course, you can stay," I said. He told me they would leave a note on the table for my sister, Bonnie, to call me for an update, as she was out with friends.

I had so many questions—what happened, how bad were his injuries, where did it happen? I hoped I would have answers by the time my sister called. I got a room ready for my parents right away, so when they called I could go to the hospital and meet them. About an hour later the phone rang again.

"Hello." I thought it was my sister. It wasn't. It was my Dad. He said two words that I'll never forget.

"Bonnie's dead."

I was stunned! How was that possible? She was supposed to be calling me. I thought they went to see my brother in the hospital. He was the one who'd been in a car accident. It made no sense.

Later that night, my father told me that my brother and sister had been in the car together with some of their friends. They were traveling to a dance when they were T-boned in a rural intersection at around 9:00 p.m. My sister, who had been sitting in the front seat, died at the scene. My brother, who was in the back seat, suffered numerous cuts and injuries to his face and neck and was going to need surgery. My parents were stunned at what had happened. They needed to stay at the hospital to be with my brother and asked if I would go out to the farm and try to get in touch with my other sister, Karen, who was away at college in another city.

I packed a bag for myself, Mike and Jennifer and we drove out to the farm. I remember walking into the kitchen and seeing the note for Bonnie on the table—I was again struck with a sense of disbelief. Was this really happening? I tried to call my sister Karen several times, and there was no answer. I started to worry that something might have happened to her too, it was two in the morning and she wasn't answering her phone. Finally, I called the police, who went to her apartment and knocked on her door waking her up, telling her to call home. I think that was one of the hardest things I have ever had to do—tell my sister that our younger sister was dead.

During the next few days, I felt like I was operating on autopilot. To this day, I don't know what I would have done if I did not have my daughter, Jennifer, to take care of. She needed me.

I helped my parents deal with all the funeral arrangements. Walking into the funeral home and looking at caskets and talking about the logistics of the funeral service and burial seemed surreal. I think my parents were struggling to keep things together. I honestly didn't know how they could do it, what it must be like to lose a daughter. I don't know what I would have done had I lost Jennifer.

The funeral was huge. The church was full and people stood outside. The procession to the cemetery was long, cars as far as I could see. And then it was all over, everyone went back home. My husband stated, "It's over now, time to go home." I couldn't go. My family needed me and I needed my family. I told Mike to go ahead without me and I would call him when I was ready to come home. I think that it was important for Jennifer and me to be there with my parents. I knew how much she was helping them with their grief.

Every day Mike would call. "You done yet?"

"Not yet," I would say. While I was away from him, I began to realize that the marriage was not right for me. My parents had been against the marriage. They didn't even come to the wedding. I was stubborn and I was going to prove that they were wrong about him. I married him against their wishes. During the time of grieving my sister's death, I began to recognize that my parents were likely right about him. I didn't know what I was going to do.

A month after my sister died, I called Mike to come and pick us up. He didn't even come into the house, he blew the horn from the driveway. When we got home he was angry and accused me of being selfish and making my family more important than him. Over the next few weeks, things became worse between us. He was drinking more and was angry all the time. He became verbally abusive and I was worried that it would become physical. I was scared. I recognized that what I was living was not what I wanted for myself or my daughter. I started thinking about what was really important to me and what I wanted for myself and for her. It was time to face the truth. The marriage wasn't working and I knew in my gut that it was never going to work. Admit to my mistake. I made plans to leave the relationship. I knew that my family would support me in whatever way they could. I began to think about how and when I would leave. Then one day, six months after my sister's death, he left for work and I called a taxi to take Jennifer and me to the train station. We caught a train and moved in with my family.

Shooting stars symbolize that a change is coming. In some cultures, it's new beginnings and in others a symbol of endings. In my case, it was both, the ending of my sister's life and the beginning of a new life for Jennifer and me.

My sister's death gave me the courage to face what wasn't working and the strength to move towards a better life for myself and my daughter. The first few years were a challenge, reflecting back on that time, I recognize how that courage lead to growth and new beginnings. Over the course of my life, when I noticed that I was in a place where I needed to make a change, I knew that I would have the courage to make that change. I quit my job to go to university and get a degree in social work. Then we left the city we'd lived in for eleven years and moved across the country to explore new opportunities. This courage has allowed me to recognize when things in life aren't working and that it's okay to move on to something new.

I now have a wonderful life. I got married again and Jennifer has a sister. They are now both married to great men. Jennifer has a beautiful family of her own and a career in education. I am getting ready to retire from my work, to follow a new path knowing that I can trust myself to recognize what isn't working and change direction if needed. Whenever I look up in the night sky and see a shooting star I am grateful that I now have the courage to recognize and face what isn't working.

Susan Brown has a Master's Degree in social work. She has worked in a variety of settings providing counseling services to those experiencing mental health challenges. She has woven together the success principles with acceptance and commitment therapy to enable clients to move forward despite mental health issues. Susan has a private practice in Calgary, Alberta, where she supports individuals, groups, and provides workshops. To contact Susan Brown please email YourReWirementforsuccess@ gmail.com.

Zoey: The Power To Choose

By Michael Maske

"The man who complains about the way the ball bounces is likely
the one who dropped it."
— Lou Holtz

My daughter Zoey was due to be born in the middle of July 2011. I was eagerly anticipating this happy event, full of dreams about how our life together would be. Everything seemed to be under control and going perfectly! I was a very successful vice president of sales for a medical equipment manufacturer and now, with career success in hand, the next chapter was about to open up for me. I had studied and immersed myself in personal and professional development, striving for life's success. Much of it I had (or so I thought), and was experiencing.

There is a concept called, *Take 100% responsibility for your life*. I thought I knew this concept, yet as I found out, life sometimes offers us a test, and the test is merely *Do you REALLY understand, or do you only THINK you understand?* For me, it was this moment that the test would present itself.

Early on July 14, 2011, Zoey's mother, Rachelle said, "Something doesn't feel quite right."

After what seemed like a very peaceful forty weeks of pregnancy, we decided to be on the safe side and have an ultrasound done. Within an hour, we were in to see a sonographer who took a quick look and noted that somewhere along the way the baby's growth had slowed, and her heart rate was oscillating between 60 and 120 beats per minute. This had quickly become a high-risk pregnancy! We were instructed to drive directly to St. Joseph's Hospital in downtown Phoenix, as they had renowned NICU facilities. The anticipation of the moment was replaced by the most intense fear and terror I have ever experienced in my heart. *Happy and healthy* was my only prayer!

Hospital specialists confirmed that the baby was in distress. Little Zoey Simone was born by C-section at 1:10 a.m. on July 15, 2011. She was whisked away to the NICU, attended by a dedicated team of nurses, doctors, and other specialists. As I sat with Zoey in the NICU that first night, already I realized how special this little girl was to me. With just one look at her, I had fallen in love. And by the miracle of God, she was healthy. She would need a feeding tube, as she had been born very small, at only four pounds, four ounces. Just a few days, and we would be on our way home.

The following day I received news that would change not only my life but, my entire view on life. Twelve hours after Zoey's birth, a physician explained that Zoey had health challenges.

He said, "We heard a heart murmur as we listened to her heart after birth. This indicated the need for some testing. We did that while you were asleep. Zoey was born with a heart defect. It is called an AV septal defect. This is a hole in the center of her heart, and it will require open-heart surgery before she is six months old."

After attempting to process the news of this serious heart defect, he said five words that would forever change my life. He wanted to be direct, to avoid any confusion on my part with regards to what he was about to say. He looked me directly in the eyes and uttered those words that would forever change the trajectory of my life.

"Your daughter has Down Syndrome." He continued, "There are certain physical features that corroborate our assessment. I'm very sorry to deliver this news, but you need to be prepared for what's ahead of you." Brusquely, he told me that Zoey would still have a normal life. And then, abruptly, he turned on his heels and left.

I guess my initial response was very human. I was stunned. A normal life? Was he kidding? An inner voice was screaming, "I don't want this reality!" There was such emptiness in my heart. And there was also fear, anger, confusion, and an overwhelming feeling of disempowerment. After all, I had spent my adult life being in control of my personal and professional destiny. I had also imagined so many things about Zoey's future. Dancing. Dramatics. Giggling girlfriends. The school honor roll. All these dreams were now shattered. Why isn't she absolutely perfect? How could this happen instead? I sat in my chair and began to cry.

Thankfully, Susan, the nurse who was caring for Zoey, heard my conversation with the physician. She pulled up a chair next to me, looked into my eyes, and just sat with me for a while.

Finally, she said, "I have a daughter who was born into this world in a similar way. She's now 24 years old." She told me about their life together, including the challenges, the victories, and the meaning that this life created. Opening up her heart to me, she began to cry as well. We sat together for a very long time, open and vulnerable, as I attempted to understand what the event of Zoey's birth meant for me.

One of the first phone calls I made was to my friend Todd Campbell, a personal development trainer/coach. I told him Zoey's story, and he immediately understood my despair.

"You had a story all made up about your future—and Zoey's," he said. "And you've just had a nuclear missile shot right through that narrative. I know you're grieving. But let me ask you this. From this moment on, how are you going to show up as a father? How are you going to show up as a man? How is Michael Maske going to show up?"

His questions were an amazing gift. In just a few words he made me realize that Zoey's future – and mine—depended on how I responded to this event. I had a responsibility to control the outcome. At that moment, I also realized that I had the power to ensure that the outcome would be great!

Since that day, I've made it my mission to be the father and the man Zoey needs me to be—caring, strong, and patient—to help her achieve success. Little did I know eight years ago that focusing on Zoey's outcome would transform both my professional and personal life—all for the better.

Today Zoey is eight years old. Over the years, doctors warned me about her limitations. "She could be like this, but she won't ever be like this."

Looking back, I'm able to say, "Great! Who cares!" For me, amazing little Zoey is beyond compare. She has taught me that she and I are much more alike than we are different—in our likes, our dislikes, and our determination. She loves almost all those things that I fantasized about eight years ago—dancing, dramatics, sports, friendships—but she masters them a little more slowly. And she never gives up. And we never give up on her, or her dreams.

As a result of our journey together, one of the best lessons I've learned is the danger of comparing any child to other children. So we compare *Zoey Today* to *Zoey Yesterday*. There's no one else in that success equation. I simply want her to be the best version of herself that she can possibly be. And with the realization that, when I take 100% Responsibility, I own the response. I don't always choose what happens in my life, but EVERY time, I have the choice—the ability to respond.

Over four years ago, I started my own medical equipment distribution business. The name that I chose for my business is ZM Medical. The ZM stands for Zoey Maske. It is a daily reminder of the power of SHOWING UP, of the power of taking 100% Responsibility, and the power that I have in the creation within my life. I'm humbled knowing that it is here that my power lies, that Zoey's power lies. And it is here that your power lies.

Michael Maske is the founder/president of ZM Medical, a medical supply/distribution company that provides healthcare facilities with innovative products that improve the safety of both healthcare staff and patients. He is a nationally known expert in safe patient handling and holds two patents on patient handling devices. He is the author of the book, Voice of the Nurse, *and advocates on behalf of nursing and patient safety issues. He is a recognized keynote speaker at healthcare conferences. Michael served in the military for twelve years, including Operation Iraqi Freedom in 2003, and is a certified Canfield Methodology trainer. He can be reached at Michael@zmmedical.com.*

LOVE REWARDS THE BRAVE

By Gwen Medved

"Life is not about negative circumstances that happen to you, it's about what you do with the golden opportunities hidden within!"
— Rhonda Byrne

"The real question is, what are you going to do now? What do you choose now? Because you can either keep focusing on that, or you can focus on what you want. And when people start focusing on what they want, what they don't want falls away, and what they want expands, and the other part disappears."
— Jack Canfield

Growing up, my home smelled of coffee, cigarettes, and legal arguments. At thirteen, there was nothing I loved more than these mornings at home. My dad, a voracious attorney would often bring his work home on weekends, dragging his law partner Pat, with him. He and Pat would sit, huddled at the kitchen table for hours, rehearsing, fine-tuning, master crafting their cases and arguments to perfection, working both sides from every angle. Sunday strategy sessions were about being prepared. Ready for what might come in the courtroom so the outcome resulted in their favor.

These were my Sunday mornings. To many girls, it might seem painful, but to me it was glorious. While other kids were riding their bikes and playing with dolls, I was buzzing around the kitchen table, where the real action was. I was helping win the next case, helping families, helping people who could not stand up alone against deep-pocketed corporations and insurance companies. There is no place I would rather have been, than at my dad's side. I'd fought hard to stay there since I was a little girl of five, which is when my mom left us. In those early days, world-class temper tantrums won me the right to spend nights and weekends with him playing in an empty office while he worked. As long as I was with my dad everything was ok, and everything would always be ok. Home with a babysitter was not an option.

One Sunday morning, there was a horrible crashing noise. I bolted upstairs to find my father flip-flopping on the floor. His eyes rolled to the back of his head. There was black blood coming out of the corner of his mouth. Fear washed over my entire body. A feeling of numbness crept over me. Frozen with stomach-turning, I watched as the paramedics carried him out to the ambulance. The only thought racing through my mind was, what will happen to me if something happens to him?

Tests showed what I witnessed was a grand mal seizure caused by absolutely nothing they could determine. Lucky for us, this revealed an AVM (arteriovenous malformation) in his brain: an aneurysm. He needed brain surgery. He was a ticking time bomb, sure to die without it.

My dad's surgical preparation was meticulous. No one was going to craft the outcome he desired unless he did everything he could to craft it himself. Game on. He must have been terrified, but he turned his fear into action and did what he did best. He prepared, and prepared to win. He researched, learning all he could, about cutting-edge procedures, searching out and finding the best newest procedures, and the most skilled surgeons in the world who would give him the best results. It was 1983. There were only two in the world. By telephone from Alaska, he secured a procedure with the one in California. I was thirteen.

My father became my greatest teacher. I saw the power of taking 100% responsibility for your own life first-hand, truly for the first time ever. I observed everything he did to prepare for his brain surgery. I heard all the questions he asked. We discussed all the logic between each choice he made. He was teaching me, coaching me, training me, demanding that I, also, learn this important lesson. His survival depended on it, and although he was not sharing his greatest fear with me, which was that he may not survive the surgery, he was teaching me this lesson now in case he was not around to teach me later.

Being an attorney, he had seen far too many cases where things went wrong unnecessarily, and learned mistakes are made innocently all the time by the best-intentioned people. Therefore, the outcomes we care most about are always up to us individually. My dad showed me how to be my own advocate. He made no excuses and placed no blame or responsibility on anyone other than himself in crafting an outcome he desired. In this moment, and any and every situation for the rest of my life, no one would ever care about my life outcomes more than I would. So, I learned the important action steps for success. Do research. Do homework. Ask questions. Get answers. Make my own determinations about what the next best steps are. Always educate myself and advocate for myself, no matter what—and to always be brave and stand up for myself in the face of adversity.

I did not know until he was fully recovered that the best stats given to him were 50:50 for life or death, with near certainty that he would lose some of his cognitive ability and use of his left arm. Those were not odds in his favor, so he did not apply them. He rejected the negative odds and worked towards the only outcome that was acceptable to him: a full recovery.

Witnessing my dad taking 100% responsibility for his life and beating the odds by doing so changed my life forever.

During the months of his recovery, we hung out a lot. I was glued to him and I was terrified of losing him. I watched him like a hawk the whole time. Those were tough days. We were edgy and uncertain. The foundation of my life was recovering from a life-threatening procedure and my future felt frightening and unknown.

One day, the sad, often overworked subject of my mom came up. In the past, sharing our mutual heartbreak and abandonment always seemed like a good way to spend some time together. We shared the same pain and, typically in the past, he was always willing to listen to my woes and then add a few of his own. I was ready to spend some good quality time bitching and moaning about her absence, but this time, he would have none of it.

My father, with nostrils flaring, and voice hard and stern, cut me off. I sat staring at the giant crescent moon-shaped scar that was just starting to heal, where they had opened up his head.

"Goose, you need to sh*t or get off the pot in regards to your mother, you really do. You need to decide if you actually want this relationship. Do you? Because it's really up to you. So decide. If no, then screw it, be done. If yes, then this, what you are doing here, is a waste of your time," he told me. "If you want it then YOU do what you need to do to make it work, and if not, then let it go. It's up to you whether your mom is going to be a part of your life or not."

I began to cry, and he pointed his finger at me to make his point stick, but his eyes were soft.

"Yep. That's right. It's YOUR choice now. You control how this is going to go down. You get to decide what you want. Think hard about that, Goose. Make a choice that is good for you. Then make it happen. I can't sit here anymore and listen to you whine and complain about what she's done anymore. Sure, it's horrible, and yeah, it hurts. I understand. I really do. But get on with life or get over it, kid. I'm sorry your mom left, but you've got me, alright? So, enough. If you're ready to move on, you've got to quit your moaning. Stop wasting so much time feeling sorry for yourself. You could eat up your whole life being a victim. Is that what you want?"

Slowly, I shook my head. No, I realized. It was not what I wanted.

I wanted a relationship with my mother but I was so scared to let her back into my life. I was afraid of more rejection. Up until this moment, I did not know that I had the power to determine outcomes. I did not know I could choose how to move forward. I had permission to decide what felt good and right. If my mom and I could not have a relationship that was positive for me, then I had the same right to walk away from it that she had. Understanding this was so powerful.

A visit was arranged with my mom. I would see her for the first time in almost five years. Holy shit. I brought my best friend with me. I couldn't do it alone. Unleashing all my new personal power on my mother, I chose to use it in the most hurtful way possible. Nothing but pure venom came out of my mouth. My words were cruel, crass, cutting, and meant to wound and destroy. Nasty as I was, and after I said every hurtful thing imaginable, tears streaming down my face, I cried until I had nothing left expecting to hear the doors slam as she left my life for the last time and for good.

My mother amazed me. When I was finally done unleashing years of silence and pent up hurt and heartbreak, she simply said, "Of course you feel this way."

And that was it. She was back in and I chose having her in my life versus not having her. It happened in an instant. Total proof that the greatest gifts can come from the worst circumstances and that love always rewards the brave. Love makes you strong and brave and powerful. It gives you the ability to do the tough things you are most afraid of. My mother loved me enough to show up for the character assassination she knew was waiting for her. I loved her enough to let her back in my life. She loved me enough to show up and try again with me. My dad loved us both enough to create a bridge, not a wall between us. There are always lessons learned when we walk bravely through our pain.

Today, taking total responsibility for myself, my health, happiness, and success has been the single common denominator in each and every success I have experienced in all areas of my life. At fourteen, I almost lost my dad, resurrected the relationship with my mother, and learned the power and success that comes from being brave, forgiving, honest, asking for what I wanted, and most importantly, loving myself enough to take control of my own happiness by taking responsibility for it myself. My dad taught me that.

Gwen Medved, M. Ed., is a success coach, bestselling author, entrepreneur, and executive producer of the film It's Happening Right Here. Gwen is a powerful strategic partner and advocate for those working to empower women and protect the rights of children. A successful product investor, and innovator, Gwen knows first-hand what it takes to create opportunity and abundance in life and business when opportunity is not handed to you. Connect with Gwen at www.gwenmedved.com.

LIFE'S A BITCH WITHOUT POKER CHIPS

By Bob Sollazzo

"Avoiding danger is no safer in the long run than outright exposure.
The fearful are caught as often as the bold."
— Helen Keller

The year was 2000. I had been living and working in Phoenix, Arizona, for a little over twenty years. An avionics company had recruited me in 1979, from Indiana, after graduating with a degree in electronic engineering. I felt successful and the future was as bright as the Arizona sunshine. I moved my wife and son to Phoenix, the land of palm trees, mountains, and opportunity. I had escaped that, "Life's a bitch and then you die," thinking that I grew up with. You know, the story where you never get ahead, and if you do, something always goes dreadfully wrong. Well, Phoenix was looking pretty darn good.

I continued taking on more and more responsibility and started working with computer technology. I found myself thoroughly enjoying the camaraderie shared with other technical professionals. Then, twelve years later, the company closed the department and laid us off. I found other jobs, but now computer technology wasn't the business, just a necessary complication. I felt tolerated at these jobs, more than valued.

Then, on a Wednesday in April 1999, I came home, dragging from a long exhausting day at work, much like the day before and the month before that. I walked in the door to find my wife of twenty-five years, my high school sweetheart, standing there, her suitcases packed. I looked at her wondering, "What now?"

She looked down at the floor and muttered that she was leaving.

I was exhausted and now feeling defeated. This was not the first time. When life was most difficult for me, she added to the drama. I mumbled goodbye and she left.

I remembered thinking that she would go somewhere for a few days, but that we would eventually work things out. That's what couples do, right? Later that week, I learned the truth. She had moved in with a guy that left his wife that same evening. I was devastated. We had just celebrated our twenty-fifth wedding anniversary in Playa del Carmen, Mexico, less than six months prior. We had, so I thought, so much fun visiting the sights, swimming and playing in the sun and surf. It had been my best vacation ever.

I had been working hard to get ahead and create more opportunities like that for us. I saw us strolling down the beach together in retirement, barefoot, hand in hand, contently looking out over the ocean, and watching the sun slowly set over a tropical paradise. Wasn't that the way it was done? You worked hard now so that you could play later?

I felt betrayed and abandoned. All hope for our future now gone, I drank myself stupid for two weeks. I didn't leave the house, didn't call in to work—for two weeks. No one called, no one came looking.

Towards the end of the two weeks, I drunkenly took a whole bottle of something to end the pain, but I woke up the next day. Failing at that, too, I cleaned myself up and went back to work. Everything there was still the same, but I was different. Empty. My self-proclaimed soulmate had abandoned me, but at least I had my job. I filed for divorce and threw myself even more into my work.

I was the IT administrator at the corporate office of a company that was struggling with IT infrastructure growth issues. This fast-growing company had offices in every major city and regional offices in Los Angeles, Chicago, and New York. I was the first computer professional hired. I was thrilled for the opportunity, but I was working long hours and had a lot of irons in the fire. The list was substantial: a financial system migration, installation of networks and servers in remote offices, company-wide email implementation, a road crew mapping system, a new phone system, and a Y2K (Year 2000) computer crash prevention project. I had taken on important, but exhausting responsibilities.

I worked hard and was rewarded. Towards the end of 1999, I asked my manager for a performance review. I planned to ask for a better salary since I was managing so much critical work for the company. My divorce was finalized in December and my review had been scheduled for the first Friday in the new year. I felt the hope of a new beginning. I went to the CFO's office on the day and time of the meeting feeling prepared to make my case. I had an outline of all the projects, their costs, and benefits to the company. I was confident. However, once at his office, I knew something was wrong. The HR manager was there and stayed for the meeting. I felt the sickening pit in my stomach grow as the CFO, my manager reminded me that the company had been sold that summer. I was aware of the sale, but my focus had been on the endless string of tasks that always needed immediate attention. He went on to say that my position had been eliminated. IT management for the company was being absorbed by the parent company. I remember the disbelief and shock as I asked if I had any options.

He said, "No." That was my last day.

I left his office dazed and confused. I expected to be rewarded for an incredible self-sacrificing effort, only to be fired. How could this happen? How could I have so many important projects and be dismissed so simply? They didn't walk me out and I was too shocked to leave. I should have left, but my ego work-ethic pride wouldn't let me. I went back to my office and created turnover notes. I thought about everything I had been through, all of those long days, and everything I was working on. In the end, it had meant nothing. They had even waited until after the new year to make sure that there were no Y2k computer failures.

I took a deep breath as I completed my notes and felt a feeling of sheer relief wash over me. The responsibility and pressure were gone. This had been the most challenging and demanding job I'd ever had. I remembered that first day on the job. I was thrown right into a huge network crisis due to a lack of planning. A communications line between the corporate and regional office was terminated, but the replacement line never came up. While I rectified the problem by the end of the day, that had set the pace. I should have quit that first day. There was never enough time and there was always another crisis. While I was feeling bruised and spent, I left work that last day realizing that it had been the best day on the job.

Though relieved to be away from that job, I also found myself in a deep depression. I was lost. My self-worth had been tied up in being a father, a husband, and a professional. Now, my son was on his own out of state, my wife had left me, and the very thing that was going to get me through was irretrievably gone. I had no close friends and had no hope that things would improve tomorrow. I didn't have the energy, confidence, or courage to look for work, and I knew that things would only get worse the longer I stayed in Phoenix.

I sold everything that wouldn't fit in a U-Haul trailer and drove back to my hometown. I had originally moved from Indiana with so much going for me, only to return a complete failure. I remember thinking how ironic it was that my ex-wife was staying in Phoenix. She had always wanted to go home, and I was going back to the place that I thought I had escaped.

This began a time of awakening for me as I reflected on how things went so wrong. What warning signs did I miss? Why had no one ever stepped in to help or warn me? I slowly began to accept the notion that everyone had their own *stuff* and it wasn't their responsibility to save me from mine. That was my responsibility. It was clear that *stuff* was always going to happen. And, suffering was dependent on my response to the *stuff*. I realized that there had been many yellow alerts over the years, but I had ignored them, hoping they would go away. The truth was, I avoided the warnings because I didn't have the courage to face flaws in my character and my relationships. I was a workaholic to avoid dealing with the problems in my life. I used labels like *work ethic, work that mattered*, and *creating a future*, but I took it to an extreme. Now, finally, I was asking myself the important questions: "Why do I keep doing that?" and "What do I really want?"

Many years have passed since those dark days. Yes, I have repeated some lessons over and over. They have been wake-up calls to practice better awareness and self-care. A few years ago, I learned about the concept of self-esteem. Self-esteem is like playing the card game poker with poker chips. We tend to *play* life conservatively when we only have a few chips and losing means the end of the game. We take more chances to win when we have plenty of chips and can afford to lose a few hands. This was the missing piece of knowledge. The following truths have totally and fundamentally changed my life forever:

- I learned that self-esteem is energy, the fuel behind healthy risk-taking courage. And, that self-esteem is not naturally occurring in the human animal.
- I learned that we all have a self-esteem *Savings and Loan* account that we are depositing into, or withdrawing from. Negative thinking, feelings, and situations withdraw from the account AND our ability to be courageous. Thoughts like, *I'm stupid, I'm ugly, I'll never get it right*, or *I'm no good at this* withdraw from our account. On the other hand, positive thinking, feelings, and situations create more self-esteem and courage. Surrounding yourself with positive supportive people, intentionally doing things that bring you joy, and practicing an attitude of gratitude creates more self-esteem and courage to win or learn.

- I learned that fear is False Evidence Appearing Real. It's the story that I told myself that scared me into staying stuck. I lived in the shadows most of my life because I lacked the courage to step out and risk failing. We don't grow if we are afraid to fail. We absolutely lose when we are afraid to play.

Now at sixty-four years old, my life is sweeter and more fulfilling than it has ever been. I invite you to seek out and learn techniques that increase your self-esteem and the self-esteem of those you love. What a profoundly simple way to improve every aspect of one's life!

"Let's remember that our children's spirits are more important than any material things. When we do, self-esteem and love blossoms and grows more beautifully than any bed of flowers ever could."
—Jack Canfield

May you and your loved ones be blessed with a never-ending supply of poker chips.

Bob Sollazzo has close to forty years as an introverted information technology professional. Progressing from troubleshooting things, to analyzing systems, to transforming himself, he believes that our greatest gifts often come disguised in heartbreak and tragedy; that the sweetest life is created when we intentionally step out of our comfort zone to create more joy, love, and success in our life and the lives of those around us. Inviting you to aim higher, he can be reached at Bob@ InspiredAim.com.

WHISPERS FROM THE UNIVERSE

By Maggie Sullivan

"You've got to ask! Asking is, in my opinion, the world's most powerful – and neglected – secret to success and happiness."
— Percy Ross

I have struggled most of my life with low self-esteem. There have been times when I have felt confident and able to handle what life throws my way with ease. Yet, I have also been haunted by a limiting belief that I was not good enough, and this belief was in the driver's seat for most of my life.

My father died when I was three, and my mother suffered from severe mental health issues. She then resorted to alcohol to ease her pain of the loss. She never remarried and never worked outside of the home. The combination of her mental health issues and addiction to alcohol left me growing up in a very dysfunctional family.

Money was tight and we would often fight about it. I wanted things, as most children do, and did not understand why I could not have the things I wanted. Our fights would escalate to a point where she would throw what little money she had at me, and tell me to manage the household—and then leave. She would walk down the street, and I would watch her walk away to a certain point. And then, the fear of being abandoned would set in, and I would chase after her, and beg her to come back. I would promise that I would be better and that I would not ask her for anything.

These fights happened frequently, until about the age of twelve. Then I made a decision to not go after her anymore. I can see now that the lack of communication and resulting fights were the beginning of a pattern that I repeated often in my adult life – not asking for what I wanted and instead, just giving up.

My teenage years continued to be difficult, with failed relationships, family arguments, and self-sabotaging behaviors. These problems continued into my twenties, with the addition of a new pattern – overworking at jobs and at school. I would spend hours every day studying, and this became a new way of life. I was unaware of what a balanced lifestyle looked like, lacked self-love, and avoided taking care of myself.

When I finished university, in an attempt to change my life and leave my past behind, I moved miles away from home. I got married, started a family, and began teaching at the local school. I loved every moment of my new job—sometimes a little too much, at the expense of spending time with my family. This overworking addiction continued as I poured myself into my work. I took extra courses to advance my career because there was no way I was going to be in a situation like my mother where I didn't have enough money to be, do, and have the things that I wanted.

It wasn't until I was in my mid-forties that the toll of working so much caught up with me. I realized that my life was passing me by, and I wasn't present to enjoy it. With that realization, I began my quest to make changes in my life. I started reading mindfulness books and the book that changed my life was Robin Sharma's *The Monk Who Sold his Ferrari*. After reading that book, I realized that there was more to life than working all of the time. My children were growing up quickly and I was not always present to enjoy it. I spent the next four years growing in self-awareness, working on healing old wounds, and becoming more present in my life. When I turned fifty, I took a year off work to spend time with my children, my husband, traveling, and learning to love myself.

I returned to work the following year with a renewed spirit. I was eager to get back and felt a calling to work with special needs students. That was one of the first times when I paid attention to the whisper from the Universe.

I also continued to deepen my self-awareness by reading great thought authors, journaling, and meditating. Every day, I felt I was getting more in touch with my authentic self. Then, I started following Jack Canfield and learned about the success principles, which helped me to understand about taking full responsibility for my life and happiness. I learned that if I want better outcomes in my life then I need to make better choices. Since finding these principles and achieving greater success in my life, I discovered that I wanted to share these principles with others.

I became a certified Success Principle trainer for Jack Canfield's work and started teaching Success Principles workshops in my basement. I eventually opened up a wellness center and offered workshops.

However, my big dream was to bring the success principles into my elementary school.

Around this time, the principal position at my school became available and I believed that this would be an excellent opportunity to share my knowledge of the success principles. I applied for the job and felt I had an excellent chance of being the successful candidate because of my qualifications, experience, and knowledge of the needs of the school. Yet, it was not meant to be.

When I found out I did not get the position, immediately I said, "Next! Something just as good or better is going to come along." When I told my husband that I was not the successful candidate, he said, "You have been given a gift—the gift of time." He was so right. I realized that it was once again the universe stepping in and whispering to me that I had some unfinished life lessons that I still needed to learn.

The following September, I continued helping students with special needs, and I took more time for myself by perfecting the art of self-care. My mother passed away the following spring and I traveled back home to spend some time with my family. At that time, I realized that there were still some lingering issues from my dysfunctional childhood that needed to be addressed, so I focused on these with a counselor.

The next fall, additional life lessons continued to emerge. I was so grateful for the support of my counselor as I worked on these lingering issues. I thought that I was making progress and had eliminated the limiting tendency toward self-doubt, and was on the road to comprehensive wellness. However, there's a funny thing about the past: unless you deal with it, really diving deep, it has a way of sneaking back into your present life. The Universe presents lessons in a variety of forms until they are truly learned. For me, a huge residual effect that resurfaced at this time was my fear of abandonment.

After working at the same school for twenty-one years, I was involuntarily transferred to a different school in a different community. I was told that changes needed to be made in the organization and I was the change. I was devastated. Every limiting belief that I ever experienced about myself came flooding back. I once again felt like the little girl whose mother had walked away from her. My fear of abandonment returned and self-doubt reared its ugly head again. This experience and the ensuing self-doubt paralyzed me. Thankfully, I had wonderful support within my learning communities and friends. But, underneath it all, I had lost all belief in myself and I no longer felt worthy. My spirit was broken. I felt abandoned, and most of all, I grieved the loss of close friends that I had known for over twenty years.

During this period of time, I had good days and bad. I continued working on my own mindfulness journey and I believe that if I hadn't been on this journey I may never have understood the lessons available to me. I refer to this period of time in my life as when my childhood trauma collided with adulthood. I truly understand that if there are any lingering effects from childhood trauma that have not been dealt with it, they come back in the form of lessons.

The following year, I decided to take early retirement from teaching at the elementary school level. I was no longer experiencing joy in my work and I concluded that life is too short to not be living in joy every day.

Unsure what my next step was going to be, I decided to enroll in Jack Canfield's *Train the Trainer Live* program and did a little bit of substitute teaching. While I was teaching in new contexts, I started to believe in myself again. I realized that I am an amazing teacher and the children where I taught loved me. This helped raise my confidence, and my belief in myself was starting to return.

My self-esteem continued to grow and I experienced a significant breakthrough during the second week of the live portion of the *Train the Trainer* program. The principles that I was given to research and present was how to be an effective asker and how to reject rejection. Researching these principles was another whisper and gift from the Universe. By studying these principles, I learned so much about the importance of asking and rejecting rejection and how improving in these two areas can increase self-esteem.

I reflected on everything—my dysfunctional family, the lack of communication between me and my mother, my fear of asking her or anyone for anything, my fear of abandonment, my low self-worth, and my fear of rejection. Studying these two principles opened the door for me to release my limiting belief of self-doubt and not being good enough.

Everything unfolded as it was meant to. My experiences, as difficult as they were, were gifts from the universe so that I could learn from these life lessons. Since this awakening, I am now in the driver's seat and I believe in myself. As each day passes, I understand more and more that our purpose in life is to be the most awakened person that we can be. I now understand that the universe sent me these gifts so that I would share my purpose with a larger platform. I do this now through sharing my stories in my books, speaking engagements, and programs. I now help others learn to become better communicators and better at asking for what they truly want so that they can experience deeper connections with others and develop greater self-awareness and inner peace. If you would like to find out more about how to create a beautiful life, visit my website at www.maggiesullivan.ca and check out my online programs.

Maggie Sullivan is a #1 Bestselling Author, certified Canfield Methodology trainer, and speaker. Maggie was an elementary teacher for over twenty years and took early retirement to fulfill her true passion for sharing her purpose of helping others deepen their self-awareness and inner peace. Maggie has inspired many people through her stories, keynote speeches, and live events. Her online programs focus on topics of everyday life and how to create and enjoy a beautiful life. To book Maggie for speaking or training: email msullivan@persona.ca or visit her website www. maggiesullivan.ca.

Finding Inner Peace
Through Goal Setting

By Mari-Liis Sallo

"If you aim for nothing, you will hit it every time."
— Zig Ziglar

"Mari-Liis, you ought to plan your day!" said my mother. She wanted me to be more focused in my daily life.

But, I thought to myself, planning is too difficult. I want to be spontaneous and free and do whatever I like. I did not want to live by a plan, nor did I understand how to create one, and why it would matter. My childhood was full of love, happiness, freedom, and play. I was not forced to do anything major, and that's the way I wanted to keep it. I wanted to become a mountain-climbing, cave-exploring Indiana Jones, traveling the world and finding hidden treasures. I figured Indiana Jones would need to study archeology to find all the hidden treasures in remote mountain caves, so I dreamed of being an archeologist.

However, my father said: "No Mari-Liis, you cannot become an archeologist! They make close to zero money."

Our family was an average Estonian family living the Estonian ideal, where you get a good education by going to a university, then you will work, work and work some more to be successful. Success is defined by how much money you make.

My father was a businessman who owned a trucking company, and my mother studied to be a pediatrician receiving her Ph.D. in public health, from the University of Tartu. She studied really hard when my brother and I were little, and later working every day, thirteen hours straight, even on vacations, not noticing her physical limits, until she was diagnosed with cancer. Within six months from getting the diagnosis, she passed away, being only forty-six years old. Her death was followed by the death of my grandparents later the same year. I was devastated. I literally felt a part of me turn black and die inside me. In my mind, I had just moved up on, what I call, the life pyramid. The life pyramid consists of a bottom layer which is me, the middle layer, my parents, and the top part, my grandparents. The life pyramid represents a safety net. No matter what happens in life, if you are at the bottom, there are people on top that cover for you unconditionally, and you are always safe. But now three people from my pyramid were gone, and I was not ready, nor trained to take full responsibility for my life.

I learned life's lessons from my parents. My father was the master of planning big, but he almost never completed what he started. When he decided to do something with great enthusiasm, he often found himself doing something else the next day. I learned from his example. First, you do the things that are easy and what you like, and then you do the things that are difficult. And you always want to do those things at the last minute! It is like when your house is on fire, you see the carpet burning, but you decide to sit on the couch for just a little while longer, because it is so comfortable, and when you see big flames soar up, you jump up from the couch, start screaming and yelling, running around and blaming others for not helping you put out that fire.

From my mother, I learned that when you work hard and devote all your resources to your work without self-care, you end up dying at the age of forty-six with cancer.

Applying these lessons, armed with no plan, a tendency to do everything important at the last minute, and a carefree, positive mindset, I moved away from my hometown, took my father's advice to learn how to make money, and went to our capital city, Tallinn, to start my first year at the University of Estonian Business School. I had no real worries financially as my father paid for my education and supported me. My *everything-will-work-out-somehow* attitude did not work well in the university environment. The teachers did not care whether I attended the lectures or not. Nobody chased me and held me accountable. Everything was completely up to me. Most of the time I was carefree, and when things got tough and deadlines hit, I ran around putting out all the fires and wondering why did I not get excellent results for my tremendous effort? It took almost five years to finish my three-year education and get my Bachelor's degree.

In 2003, I met and began dating an extremely private and enigmatic twenty-six-year-old international motorsport driver, who was a rising star in his field. As our lives together unfolded, we were traveling extensively, first for his work and later just for fun. We have two wonderful children, Frederik and Kiara, who we love unconditionally and who bring joy to our life. All of my financial needs were met, and our relationship was very good. However, although I have a blessed life, I began feeling that something was missing. I saw my friends and peers advancing in their careers and accomplishing their life goals, but I was somehow stuck and not being fulfilled. I began searching for meaning and reading about what successful people do to reach their goals. I saw that there are people who are financially successful and happy without working themselves to death, which is the Estonian way. I discovered the first step is to find out what you really want and what will bring you fulfillment. For me, I have a passion for helping people live healthier and happier lives through holistic nutritional coaching. I have been advising my friends and supporting their healthier lifestyles, so why couldn't I leverage that knowledge to make a living and have success in my own right? I discovered the power of setting goals and committing to them until they are accomplished.

Before this discovery, I was extremely good at making excuses on why I could not do something or be who I wanted to be. In 2015, I started to awaken and finally steer my own life. I set various goals that were not too big at first. For example, I set a goal to walk five kilometers daily with my baby daughter. I delegated the housekeeping tasks to a professional, began studying at The Institute for Integrative Nutrition with a goal to achieve a certificate in health coaching, and decided to become certified in the Canfield Methodology for more specific transformation. I mended some relationships and tied up loose ends in my life. Personal goals are different for everybody. Meaningless things for some are valuable to others. That is why we always should listen to ourselves first. The one thing I never want to do is stay still and not be able to learn new things. I have found the meaningful work I want to do and I want others whom I see struggling to get the support they need for a prosperous life.

I agree with Robin Sharma that successful achievers have high levels of commitment, discipline, resilience, and perseverance. Clearly, I needed to grow my perseverance muscle. And I can tell you, this is a tough one! Remember my spontaneous nature? My brain will figure out something super exciting for me to do just when I need to stay focused and work through a difficult problem. My brain tries to distract me in a hundred ways, feeding me information on what minor tasks I need to do right that moment when I need focus and perseverance the most. A close friend of mine said, "When you don't work on a problem until it is solved, it will come and hunt you down at the most inconvenient of times." How many times has your computer crashed when you promised to do the backup tomorrow, or people come over when you just wanted to clean up but didn't, or left some important paperwork to the last minute and rushed to the airport almost missing your plane? Perseverance is a muscle that needs to be consciously grown, along with discipline, commitment, and resilience.

By setting goals and practicing perseverance, I was able to purchase my first apartment and start a new career path in coaching. My relationships and mental well-being have tremendously improved due to investing money and time in myself. Because of dreaming, setting goals, taking action, and sticking to the commitments I made, I have progressed in two years to a level where I can help others to achieve what they want. I can see the patterns, limiting beliefs, and early childhood conditioning in fellow Estonians, and I intend to change our country's mindset to a more positive and happier one.

Health is so important to me and I truly feel happy when I can see the amazing results my clients make with a little support, listening, and attention from me. If one person can have a positive impact on another person, imagine if all the people found happiness and peace within themselves and impacted the whole world.

We can be impacted and inspired by extraordinary people in our life as well as those who will not always support us, but challenge us to find and achieve the greatness inside of us. Growth also can mean some painful moments. A successful life is not always about taking the easy route. It's okay to be uncomfortable. Choosing your goals, and having discipline for as long as it takes to achieve what we want will make us successful.

Mari-Liis Sallo is a certified (IIN) Integrative Nutrition Health coach who is passionate about self-development, healthy habit formation, and building a life full of love and joy. Mari-Liis holds a BA from Estonian Business School and is a certified Canfield Transformational Trainer. You can follow her on Instagram https://www.instagram.com/mlswellness/, or write to her via email: mariliissallo@me.com.

Life Long Commitment

By Ryan Abitz

"Those who improve with age embrace the power of personal growth and personal achievement and begin to replace youth with wisdom, innocence with understanding, and lack of purpose with self-actualization."
— Bo Bennett

I grew up in Fond du Lac, WI, a small blue-collar town in the Midwest. My parents were classic products of the 1950s: high school education, meat and potatoes lifestyle, large families of siblings. My father got a job at a factory as a maintenance man when he turned eighteen and worked there until he retired at sixty-five. My mom was a homemaker for the majority of her adult life, and she spent most of her time raising me and my older brother Tony. From the beginning, my family lived the concept of *constant improvement*. My parents bought a 100-year-old fixer-upper on two-and-a-half acres a few miles out of town. They demolished and remodeled one room at a time. It was years before the family got around to replacing the siding and the roof. That pretty much defines *never-ending*! With only one income, home remodeling costs, and grocery bills, there wasn't much money left over for luxuries, or even just going out to eat.

While my friends were getting cool gifts and expensive vacations, oftentimes I couldn't even get a ride into town, because car use was rationed to get Dad to work and Mom to the grocery store. One time I asked for $5 to go to the skating rink with my friends. My parents told me, "It's not that we don't want you to go. We just don't have the money."

Incidents like that made me resent my parents at the time, but in reality, they have always been very kind people. They taught me a lot about being humble, maybe without knowing it. Their example taught me how to work hard to achieve important goals. Nothing is just handed to you. This work ethic is the foundation of who I am today.

At age ten my quest for personal self-improvement began with music! My parents saved and bought me a used guitar and amp. I would get home from school and just play guitar all night long. During the summers, I would play all day and night. There was so much to learn! But what would it take to constantly get better? Of course! A job washing dishes at a restaurant gave me the cash to buy better guitar equipment. The restaurant job opened up another avenue for self-improvement. To get out of the dish pit, I studied the line cooks. At sixteen I legally started cooking and remained a line chef until age twenty-three.

Then a friend from middle school mentioned an apprenticeship program for chefs just thirty minutes north. You mean there's something better than flipping burgers? Sign me up! With fifty/sixty-hour weeks, the apprenticeship program was an enormous amount of hard work. It was at this point in my life I really started to stretch myself and get out of my comfort zone. I moved to Wisconsin's Fox Valley and took a job in a fancy restaurant. This changed my view of food and my life forever!

Before too long, I was invited to open an Italian restaurant from the ground up. The owner of this establishment allowed his twenty-three-year-old son to run it. The doors closed six months later. Turns out, spending all the profits on excursions to the local strip club wasn't a good business model. Afterwards, my co-worker and friend Jeff ('Chefry') and I were invited to open up an Italian-destination restaurant a little farther out in the boonies. We built a great business for the owners, but ultimately, after two and a half years of more fifty/sixty-hour working weeks, we both had enough and moved on.

In the winter of 2009, I took my first vacation to sunny Austin, TX. On the drive down, an amazing feeling went right through me. Suddenly I knew I would be closing the Wisconsin chapter of my life. A week of wearing flip flops and shorts in Austin, a city full of beautiful women and great music, was all it took. I was ready to move there permanently. My goal? To start a personal and private chef business. Successful people make decisions quickly!

Back home, I put a laser focus on attaining my Austin dream. I scoured Craigslist for jobs and mapped out the city. I printed out thirty copies of my resume, packed up my Sat-u-lac (fully loaded 2001 Saturn Cadillac), and headed south, driving twenty-four straight hours to get to Austin as soon as possible. I drove from restaurant to restaurant right away, applying for a job. The third place I stopped at hired me on the spot. I had taken the first step toward creating my professional dream. But I had zero experience actually owning or operating a business. I just dove in and learned along the way.

Joining Business Networking International (BNI) made a huge difference. There, I met an accountant who set up an LLC for me and did my taxes and a website designer who made me look like a legitimate business owner. But the biggest impact was meeting a business coach who introduced me to an entirely different way of looking at life. She taught me that two+two=four. In other words, everything adds up. My choices in the past made me exactly what I am today. I attract everything into my life.

This revelation blew me away. All of these life experiences were part of my path toward personal and professional development.

Want another manifestation of constant and never-ending improvement? I became hooked on entrepreneurship. While in Austin, I built not only a personal/private chef business but also a food trailer and meal-delivery business. I then moved to Portland in 2015 to open up a meal-delivery business there. I spent my time constantly learning more about business and creating systems to improve the bottom line. I also attended workshops regularly on topics such as money mastery. In the midst of moving to Austin and starting businesses, I got wrapped up in a toxic relationship. I was so high on life due to how everything was falling into my lap, I was completely blind and ignorant about this person whom I dated for four years. As with most relationships, things start off super fun and it's easy, for me at least, to look right over the yellow alerts and not see them until they are screaming bloody red alerts! This was me!

This turned into a nightmare with false friends, crazy parties, and a girlfriend who was addicted to pills and then later, heroin. I was so caught up in being a successful business owner and having a ton of fun, I didn't realize how manipulative my girlfriend was. Slowly, I was losing my money, losing my business, and needing to relocate to Portland, Oregon because of an unknown situation involving the police and my girlfriend in which she needed to get out of Dodge. She sold me on how cool Portland was, so we took a trip up there and ended up moving there shortly after. I didn't realize exactly what was wrong with her, or that I'd been so manipulated. Two and a half years after moving to Portland, I had her physically removed from my property with a restraining order. A few nights before, she held a sharp chef's knife to my throat and threatened to kill me. We'd had fights in the past, but never that life-threatening.

I left that night and stayed with a friend of mine who asked me if I had thought to Google *Borderline Personality Disorder.* As soon as I looked it up, I found a checklist and she hit EVERY checkmark. Suddenly, everything made sense! The next morning I filed a restraining order and she was removed the following day. Shortly after, I was contacted by a sheriff in Texas wondering if I knew where she was and if I had any information on her regarding a fraud charge against her. I didn't. I still have not spoken to or seen her to this day. Out of all of this came the most beautiful gift the Universe has given me—my wife. If I hadn't followed the psycho to Portland, I doubt I would have ever crossed paths with her.

My wife is a mental health therapist (no, not the one I saw after the traumatic relationship) and brings out only the best in me. It's amazing. We never fight, occasionally have small disagreements that get talked out, not screamed at (what a concept!). We both listen to each other intently, and if we don't understand what we are saying to each other, we ask for it to be said in a different way. I have the utmost respect for my wife, and she gives me that back.

She also supports my entrepreneurial spirit while trying to create multiple streams of income. Some ventures work, some don't. For example, I burnt out from cooking, and spent a year in the solar industry, while starting a voiceover business. Although, I have found my way back to food by starting up a hydroponic microgreens business and providing my personal and private chef services to the Portland/ Vancouver metro areas.

For me, constant and never-ending improvement will always be at the core of how I live my life. And as a certified Success Principle coach in the Canfield Methodology, I love inspiring others to successfully find their unique personal and professional journey.

Ryan Abitz currently resides in Salmon Creek, WA with his wife and is a certified trainer in the Jack Canfield Methodology and Success Principles. He is also involved with the Portland, OR, Music Community, is a voiceover artist, a personal/private chef of twenty years, a microgreens horticulturalist, and is currently learning the healing properties of essential oils. Contact Ryan at RyanAbitzVO@gmail.com or visit his website www.ryanabitz.com.

CAUSE OF MY DEATH

By Wendy Witt

"Imagination is everything.
It is the preview of life's coming attractions."
— Albert Einstein

It was March 7, 1994, when I came within seconds of dying. At age twenty-eight, I was at my fourth-grade weight, my toes had evidence of frostbite, and I could no longer walk or even sit up. My veins were collapsing, metabolic acidosis reigned as my kidneys could no longer keep up, and no blood pressure was measurable. I heard the code being called and wondered what that meant and who that was for. All I knew, while laying on that ER table, was that I was *sooooo* cold and the people around me were very busy. The doctor later reported he thought he was going to lose me. I was that close to death.

During my twenties, I suffered long-term exposure to stress. That is the official medical explanation for my diagnosis: primary adrenal insufficiency (aka Addison's Disease). Because I didn't have the skills to deal with seemingly endless stress, cortisol was my body's continuous response—to the point of adrenal exhaustion—which means death.

Living alone in a new town and responsible for my financial survival for the first time, I was attending law school where you're taught how to see everything that's wrong with the world. Once that law-school world-view filter is inserted, each conversation, action, and situation contains liability or inconsistency that must be corrected. World problems felt personal.

Around that same time, my mother joined a doomsday cult, became even more manipulative, and married a stranger because she was told to, later cutting herself off from all family and friends, including my sister and me. She was sure the world was going to end and, to be saved, she and everyone else had to do exactly what they were told by the cult leaders, who pretended to receive their instructions from "the counselors." The cult leader told me that I shouldn't have children because I would not be able to feed them.

My college best friend, roommate, and friends had all taken different paths. This was the days before the Internet and cell phones, so I felt alone—and scared that I would be out on the street if I couldn't pay my bills. Overwhelmed by academic demands, my new law-school-fostered perspective, and my mother's doomsday predictions, the world became very heavy.

Then, my soon-to-be husband's mother was diagnosed with stage four cancer. Two weeks later, his father died. At ages twenty-two and twenty-three, Joe and I became caretakers with much interfamily conflict and a loss of what I thought life should be.

I knew from my studying days that using positive visualization was a successful strategy. I saw myself in *the zone* for my tax law exam.

I even had a vision board for law school graduation, with a photo of a smiling me as I graduated from high school, then college, and with a space for my law school graduation photo.

So, I knew that visualizing what I wanted academically worked. What I didn't know at that time was that visualizing what I *didn't* want also worked. I'm sharing my story with you so that you're not still paying the price for replaying fear, anger, resentment, and frustration twenty-five years later.

Where do you want to be twenty-five years from now?

Our brain doesn't know the difference between when we're going through a stressful situation and when we're just thinking about it. The body responds to the brain's stress signals and produces cortisol, a stress hormone. Overproduction of cortisol, such as caused by rumination of upsetting situations, has devastating results. For me, the results were near death and a life living with a chronic illness that few understand.

Visualization has been popular in athletics for decades. Back in the day, my husband, Joe, used pre-game imagery to become an all-star running back. He broke six university records. While he was warming up for each game, he would *see* himself catching the ball and carrying it across the goal line.

I've had to adjust my life as I'm sensitive to stress—noise, lights, people, temperature. Thus, I'm more withdrawn than I was meant to be. I seek to protect myself and limit stress, both physical and emotional.

Because of this fundamental medical issue, I've learned to catch my thoughts and to focus on what I want, not what I don't want. I have used healthy, emotionally packed visualization with action to create what I want: solid relationships with my husband, children, and friends; cash flow; professional impact; and The Happen House, the house of my dreams.

Joe and I invested in The Happen House to provide an amazing home for our family and a place for lawyers to gather who want *to make it happen*. Being an attorney is highly stressful, and many of my colleagues go through their own struggle because of the filter law school installed, as well as the emotional and physical demands prevalent in the practice of law. I help lawyers develop their business strategy and success skills, as well as the mindset, to create the law firm that gives them the life they love. Healthy, emotionally charged visualization has been a key to happiness, success, and wellness—my own and my clients'.

One of my favorite quotes is that of Einstein: "Imagination is everything. It is the preview of life's coming attractions." I created a vision board ten years ago and included this quote. Some time ago, I paged through that notebook packed with photos and words representing what I wanted to achieve, as well as inspirational quotes (including Einstein's imagination quote). I've achieved everything that I've worked for.

On June 1, 1991, I graduated from law school. Joe and I had gotten married just two weeks earlier. Now, almost thirty years later, I can see in my mind's eye, my black-and-white polka dot dress and my absolute shocked misery because, at the last minute, my mother refused to attend my graduation (as she'd been told to do so by those cult leaders). Education was highly valued in my family, so for her to abandon me was devastating. I couldn't speak. In my files is a certified letter stating I was never to contact my mother again. I received that letter in the first month of my first pregnancy. She doesn't know my children or the person I've become.

When I'm pulled to the emotions of those times I've described, or when I have other negative thoughts and fears, I intentionally pull myself to a different image, such as one of me joyfully being an incredibly awesome mother to my three children, or celebrating that my mortgage has been paid in full. These images in my mind are ones I choose, and I choose to be happy and healthy and to create the life I love.

As a result, I feel better for it. My happiness level is determined by the thoughts I think and the images I see—and I choose good ones. I invite you to do the same.

Wendy Witt, JD is the founder of Million Dollar Attorney®, a private consulting firm designed to help lawyers prosper. Her mission is to tilt the legal universe toward wellness and she does that by serving as a Master Law Firm Business Strategist who helps solo and small law firm owners build law firms that give them the life they love. Wendy is a former 15-year trusts and estates attorney who helped families with estates up to $500 million, an ABA published article author, and former national attorney organization senior executive. Her guidance has been published by Forbes, ABC, NBC, CBS, Fox, Huffington Post, Experts Institute, Solo Practice University, Pennsylvania Bar Institute, Pennsylvania Bar Association, the Pennsylvania Lawyer, among others. You can reach Wendy at Wendy@MillionDollarAttorney.com.

Hold Tight to Your Goal and You'll Steady Your Soul

By Marilyn Montgomery

"Instead of worrying about what you cannot control, shift your
energy to what you can create."
— Roy T. Bennett

It's a common practice in sports or yoga to begin each practice session by bringing an intention to mind. The intention is in service of a longer-range goal in view, such as qualifying for a next-level achievement. Why? When we set intentions for our actions each day, and we are clear about the goal they will serve, we are much more likely to align all the parts of ourselves to achieve them.

I love learning about the many theories of counseling and psychotherapy—and yes, there are many of them! This may seem nerdy, but I really and truly love going in-depth and really trying to understand the various theories. I'm always asking, "How does it work?" So, about a decade ago, I approached a friend of mine, Jeffrey Kottler, about doing a book together on theories of counseling and therapy. And we did: it was titled *Theories of Counseling and Therapy: An Experiential Approach*. It was loved by our students and adopted by many universities for use in their courses.

Fast forward a few years—the book needed to be updated. My co-author and I needed to come up with a new edition with information about the most recent research and changes in the field. But it was going to be a lot of work, and we weren't sure we wanted to commit to it. We agreed to talk about it over coffee when we were both attending an upcoming professional conference in San Francisco. Then, my husband Bill had a stroke, just three weeks before I was scheduled to speak at the conference in San Francisco.

Bill's stroke sent my world into a tailspin. I woke up early one cold, dark, Sunday morning in February, and he was moving around erratically and talking gibberish—much more incoherently than his usual morning musings. I instantly sprang to full alertness as I realized that this was a symptom of a stroke! I quickly did the mental math and figured out that I was his best chance at survival. Our rural home on a mountaintop in Pennsylvania was hard for others to find and waiting for an emergency dispatch would waste valuable time. I threw some clothes and a coat on both of us, got us into our jeep, and sped over the snowy dark road to our nearest regional hospital.

Once there, I learned that, yes, this was indeed a stroke in progress. The local hospital got an expert on webcam to do an assessment, and the surgeon delivered the news about the recommended treatment and prognosis: we could do nothing, and the stroke would continue cutting off oxygen to essential parts of the brain—but Bill might survive. Or we could risk a thrombectomy to remove the clot and restore blood flow.

By then my daughters were with me to hear the two options, each of which had an equal probability:

1) do nothing, and let the stroke run its course, which could kill him or at a minimum render him helpless,

2) perform the surgery to remove the blood clot, which could also kill him, render him a helpless person whom we would not really recognize, or give him a shot at recovering himself.

Through tears, we debated the options but quickly came to an agreement. We told the surgeon, "Do all you can to save him with the surgery."

We had to wait for hours, which seemed like an eternity. As the enormity of how this event was changing our lives began to sink in for each of us, we began pondering a larger existential question: if he survives, how will we know he is himself—the same man we loved and knew so well?

Hours later we had the news that he had survived the surgery and would be coming back to consciousness soon. We gingerly walked into the room. Would he be himself, or someone that none of us recognized, but in a familiar body? As he began to look at us and speak and gesture, we glanced at each other with enormous relief and gratitude: It's him! He's back! He survived!

Of course, that was just the beginning of our *new normal*. First, there were 24/7s in the ICU at the hospital. Then there were 24/7s at the rehab facility. All the while, I was stealing minutes here and there to keep up with work deadlines and searching for hotspots for webcam meetings and websites to help me understand his prognosis. It was exhausting, draining. But most of all, I wondered, what did this mean for my future? Everything had turned upside down. I was clueless. What about all my goals and dreams, now that Bill needed a full-time caregiver? I felt paralyzed, but my family urged me to go ahead and attend the conference in San Francisco. "You already paid for this," they said. "And you desperately need a break!"

They were right. So, I went. Jeffrey Kottler, my friend and co-author, was the keynote speaker for the conference, and it inspired me to see him connecting with the audience in the way that he does so well. I had made a date to connect with him at a coffee shop shortly afterward.

"So, are we going to do this new edition of our book, or not?" he said.

"I'm still on the fence."

"We can only do it if you really want to."

I took a deep breath and reached down into my soul and looked him in the eyes. "Yes. I want to do it." Even as I said this, I felt like I was jumping off the high dive—I had no idea how I would get this done, given my new reality. I didn't even know what the new reality would be like for me.

Always a pragmatist, Jeffrey challenged me. "You want to do it or, you want to commit to doing it? Our editor at the publishing company needs to know, yes or no, so she can write up the contract— with a deadline."

"Yes. Let's do it!" were the words that sprang from my mouth. I had no idea how I'd find the time or energy, but I committed to it.

"Then I'll write to our editor, let her know, and let's get started! I've been thinking about a new chapter we need to add on neurobiological approaches." That's all it took to get him started.

It took more than that for me to get started and to sustain my dream. Many times, when I thought of how much work it would take to reach our goal of having a fully revised and completed book to our editor by her deadline, I trembled inside. But the goal was crystal clear—it had a deadline, and I was accountable to my co-author and publisher. I had a vision for the book too, seeing it generating lively discussions in classrooms, and even accompanying some of the students as bubble-bath reading (a setting a student had confessed to me as her favorite place to read the earlier version!). I chunked it down, chapter by chapter, section by section, and stole away an hour here, there, working in coffee shops and airplanes, until we got it done.

Two years later, my vision of a colorful, inviting, new edition of the book became a reality. I was at the same professional conference I had been at two years prior, where I made the commitment to my coauthor to complete the new version of our book. Only this time, the conference was in New Orleans.

I had set another goal that was also realized that day. Through careful and extensive logistical planning, I had Bill by my side in this favorite city that we had often visited in our pre-stroke life together. We walked through the exhibit hall together, searching for the display of the publisher—and, at last, I could see it. Beneath a banner announcing *New Arrivals!* was a stack of our new book. On each cover, along with the book's title and our names as authors, was an original watercolor of a person's face in silhouette. Streams of aqua, green, rose, and gold flowed out of the top of the head, perfectly representing the beautiful energy and variety that I believe defines our human experience. In the memorable photos taken that day, Bill is on my left and I'm holding the book on my right; our smiles reflect the joy of both goals becoming a reality.

Dr. Marilyn Montgomery is a professor, author, mentor-coach, speaker, and founder of Wellspring Development. She has long been involved in scholarly research, publishing in a number of scientific journals, and is the past-president of The International Society for Research on Identity. With an interest in fostering positive development and mental health across the lifespan, Dr. Montgomery has published books for parents and counselors, including Theories of Counseling and Therapy: An Experiential Approach. She is also a Certified Canfield Trainer, Barrett Certified, and a Certified RIM Essentials (Regenerating Images in Memory) facilitator. Contact Marilyn at marilynmontgomery@me.com.

Patience, Persistence and Perspiration

By Filissa Caserta

"Patience, persistence and perspiration make an unbeatable
combination for success."
— Napoleon Hill

In Brooklyn, NY, on May 29, 1965, I came smiling into this world. I
was the fourth of five children and my older siblings were two, four,
and five years of age at the time of my birth. Yes, my poor mother. A
few years after my arrival, we crossed the Verrazano Bridge with all
of the other Italian Americans, and I spent the rest of my childhood
on Staten Island. I was a very happy child with a playful spirit and a
vivid imagination. My siblings and I were blessed to be surrounded by
children our age and in a neighborhood with such little traffic that we
could play in the streets for hours without ever seeing a car. While life
was joyful for us outside of the house, inside was a very different story.

On most nights my siblings and I would be woken up from our deep slumber by this raving lunatic woman in our kitchen screaming at my father. You see, my father, the handsome, successful, charismatic, and brilliant engineer was also a maintenance alcoholic. My mother's lack of knowledge regarding the disease of alcoholism, coupled with incredibly high-stress levels from basically raising the five of us by herself, left her with limited coping skills. So, she yelled, she threatened, yet nothing changed. I resolved to do everything in my power to prevent her from yelling and one key way was by doing well in school.

When I was a junior in high school, while in the middle of taking the New York State trigonometry regents exam, I noticed another student working on a graph that I had not yet started and was unfamiliar to me. I felt this immediate uneasiness in my stomach and started to think, "Oh my God. I don't know that one. I am going to fail." My mind began racing, as the fear that had gripped my stomach increased. I tried to go back to the problem I was working on, but I couldn't remember anything. I looked back at the other student's paper to see if maybe I was mistaken and noticed the teacher looking at me. My anxiety escalated as I realized she thought I was cheating. I raised my hand and stammered, "C… c… c… can I go to the bathroom?"

She said yes, and just as I got to the door, I passed out into the hallway. I was sixteen years old and had experienced my first panic attack. After that event, my mother pleaded with me to stop putting such pressure on myself. Neither of us understood my pathologic need for perfection, nor the impact it would have on my life going forward.

The drive for perfection, and the anxiety created when I couldn't meet my own high standards, manifested itself in a variety of other ways, including a significant public speaking phobia. When I was nominated by my fellow students to give the commencement speech at our nursing school graduation I was simultaneously honored and petrified. However, with legs that felt like wet fettuccini, I walked on the stage and, in front of my fellow nursing students, our families, and all of the school of nursing faculty, I delivered a witty and heartfelt speech. Afterwards, students and faculty alike bombarded me with praise and gushed on about how phenomenal the talk was. One of my professors gave me a hug and said, "This is your gift and you must do this professionally." I smiled and nodded as I thought, there is no way in hell I am doing that again!

I successfully avoided standing on stage until graduate school. It seemed as soon as I had the MSN credential after my name, the invitations to present on my specialty flowed in. I can recall with astonishing clarity sitting on my bed and reading an email invitation to co-lead a national project as if it was yesterday. Part of the project included presenting at a national meeting. My initial response was one of excitement. However, that excitement quickly waned as my stomach flip-flopped and every voice in my head screamed in unison, "They are out of their mind!" and "No freaking way!" However, through the din of all the protestations, there was this soft voice saying, "I think you should do it." The committee in my head proceeded to tell the voice, "You are f...g crazy! Don't you remember what it was like?" But as I, like a child, mentally held my hands over my ears saying, "La la, la la, I'm not listening." the quiet voice gently nudged me and said, "I need you to trust me, because if you do this, many doors will open for you." For some reason, those words quieted the barrage of negativity and, before I could lose my nerve, I responded with an emphatic, "Yes, I will participate."

Choosing to listen to that voice opened many doors for me, and I went on to lecture nationally and internationally for the next fifteen years. During all of that time, I intermittently battled with public speaking anxiety that actually, on three occasions, escalated to the point of my having a full-blown panic attack and passing out on the stage. But, true to my character, I did not let that deter me from giving the planned presentation. I just picked myself up, gave the talk, and walked away with a smile on my face and shame and embarrassment in my heart. I eventually decided to stop speaking, stating it was because I was tired of lecturing on the same topic, but the truth is I was done dealing with my anxiety. It had won.

Many years later, while searching through on-demand programming for something inspirational, I came across Oprah Winfrey's *Super Soul Sunday*. The episode that chose me was an interview with Jack Canfield, and he was discussing the release of the tenth-anniversary edition of *The Success Principles* book. I immediately downloaded the audiobook and started listening. I subsequently attended Breakthrough to Success live, and while I was there, learned that I could become a certified trainer. I knew this was the perfect opportunity for me, so I signed up. As I was completing the paperwork for the program, that all too familiar gnawing sensation in my gut appeared and I was struck with the limiting belief that my anxiety would prevent me from going forward with this exciting opportunity. Fortunately, I was in the space of feeling the fear and doing it anyway, so I signed the dotted line and got my cool t-shirt.

By the time I arrived at the first live Success Principles training session, I was raring to go. You can therefore imagine how devastated I was when doing a simple ninety-second introduction on day one caused me to have so much anxiety that I was two seconds away from passing out and had to sit on the stage to finish my introduction. I don't recall what I said, nor did I notice the standing ovation that my fellow students gave me as I managed to get up and walk off the stage. What I do recall is that I was again filled with shame and embarrassment. I wanted to run out of the room and never show my face to those people again.

However, that damn $E+R=O$ kept flashing through my mind. Being aware that it was my response (R) to the event (E) that governed the final outcome (O), I knew that if I ran away, the outcome would invariably be me giving up on my newly found dream. My response to the event (anxiety and panic with public speaking in the not too distant past) was to stop speaking and the outcome would mean that I was no longer sharing my gifts and talents and transforming nurses' lives. If I wanted a different outcome I had to change my response. So, I stayed in my seat for the remainder of the session, but as soon as we broke for lunch I went back to my room and sobbed. I didn't even want to go to lunch. I felt like I couldn't look at anybody. I figured that they were all judging me, and I couldn't bear it. I sat quietly for a few minutes and then decided I needed to put my big girl pants on. So I jumped up, washed my face, and joined my peers for lunch.

I was still feeling quite guarded when I entered the hall where lunch was being served, but to my surprise, people came up to me and thanked me for my vulnerability. They told me what I had done had given them courage. I smiled and thanked them for sharing but I couldn't really take it in. I had this negative thought, "Glad I could help you, but now I feel like shit." It was not until the next day, during the morning silent hug session, that my icy wall of self-protection melted. With each subsequent hug and look of love that came through my fellow trainees' eyes, I once again felt that I belonged. That the only person judging me was me and that was something that I would need to address.

When I returned for the second live training, my anxiety level was pretty manageable since I was well prepared to present the assigned fifteen-minute talk to my small group of fellow students and assistants. However, my low-level anxiety quickly changed to near panic when I found out there would be a group project that would entail me getting on stage and presenting to all of the students, the Canfield Training Group leadership team and, none other than, Jack Canfield himself. Here was a great opportunity to apply everything I had learned about overcoming obstacles and facing my fear in order to pursue my passion. So why did I feel like packing my bags and getting on the next plane home?

While at the initial planning dinner with my group, I shared my history of panic attacks and said that while I was trying not to put out into the universe the vision of me falling flat on my face on stage before I even opened my mouth, there was a possibility that it could happen. I asked them to promise me that they would not call 911 if I did pass out and explained how things would unfold, which included my quickly regaining consciousness and finishing the presentation. They listened with love and sensitivity. One of the members, who was no stranger to anxiety himself, excitedly offered the suggestion that I should share my anxiety story as part of my presentation. After resisting the temptation to slap him, I took a deep breath and thought, he's right.

It seemed like my willingness to be vulnerable and share my story as part of my presentation set the tone for the entire group and as each member shared their experience with overcoming their own obstacles, tears started streaming down my face. The universe had conspired FOR me and hand-delivered the perfect team of co-presenters. A true team that surrounded me with such love and acceptance that I was able to not only remain conscious during the entire presentation but to shine. The feedback that I would go on to receive from all participants and the Canfield team, was overwhelmingly positive.

Filissa Caserta is board certified as an acute care nurse practitioner, a neuroscience registered nurse, Level I reiki practitioner, and is certified in the Success Principles and Canfield Methodology. Her clinical acumen, passion for learning, and determination have led her to have many wonderful opportunities along her thirty-two-year nursing journey. Her entire career has been dedicated to guiding and supporting nurses. Whether teaching advanced diagnostics to acute care nurse practitioner students or guiding a new grad nurse that she met at a coffee shop, she is always willing to give of her time and energy to help her peers excel. She is the co-founder of Nurse Whisperers and can be reached at nursewhisperers@gmail.com.

The Adaptable Girl

By Ati Rahbani Rexroad

Adaptable (/əˈdæp.tə.bəl/)
adjective
Able or willing to change in order to suit different conditions.

"Adaptability is not imitation.
It means power of resistance and assimilation."
— Mahatma Gandhi

As long as I can remember, there was one word everyone used to describe me: adaptable. When I was a small child in England, my parents said it with pride, other adults with awe, and my friends' parents with a wistful longing. It seemed like such a good thing, this big word. Adaptable. A little girl who had already lived on two continents by the age of four; been exposed to cultures she couldn't name; and spoke, in some measure, three languages. So much exposure, so early in life. As I grew older, I internalized this perception of adaptability and identified with it.

I don't know exactly when I learned about those fascinating creatures that could completely adapt to their environment and situation, but I remember well relating to and thinking of myself as a chameleon. I wasn't aware of it, to be sure, but I found myself subconsciously assessing each situation and figuring out what I thought was the perfect *skin*. I wore these skins well and adapted accordingly.

As soon as I could read, I became a voracious reader. I was always curious and loved to learn. Quick to raise my hand at school, I was labeled a "know-it-all" by my English primary school (elementary school in the US) classmates. I knew it was meant as an insult, but I think, even then, I wondered why it would be so bad to "know-it-all." To my mind, it seemed a fine thing to which anyone should aspire. The adaptable girl who liked to learn. That was my adopted persona: popular with teachers, always seated in the front of the class, always behaving appropriately for the situation. And I was proud of myself.

When my family moved to the US in my tweens, I assimilated easily, if not always willingly, to changes between the UK and the US. (I stubbornly persisted in spelling *colour* with a *u* long after I knew the American spelling). I held on to my British accent as long as I could—the last outward vestige of my "Englishness"—but even that was gone by the time I was fourteen and surrounded by American friends, TV, and Ferris Bueller.

Academic testing had placed me three years ahead of grade, so I went to class with older kids in the small church school I attended. I had always had a very supportive family, and I was happy. I loved and was loved fiercely by my parents and my younger sister in kind. In my junior year, I transferred to a small private school, which my parents could only afford due to an academic scholarship. I liked school and was content, but I was acutely aware that I was younger, and I had few real friendships in my grade. I couldn't drive. I wasn't interested in drugs or sex. I was just "the young one."

I graduated high school at fifteen, just shy of my sixteenth birthday. I knew my family was proud of me, and I knew my early graduation was considered an accomplishment. I felt pride, but what I remember most is simply thinking how great it was that I wouldn't have to be driven to university in the fall.

At university, I quite enjoyed the anonymity large classes afforded, while I also relished the small class size of my honors program courses. Everyone assumed I was eighteen, so my age was no longer a topic of conversation. Neither was my desire to learn all I could. I adapted easily to each situation I was in at university. I was ever the chameleon; the social butterfly when needed; the quiet, studious girl when that suited the situation. I had a few varied groups of friends, mainly rooted in our love of similar music. I was invited to group outings and participated some of the time.

Yet I found myself wondering why I sometimes felt invisible. Not literally, but often just such a part of the fabric that conversation and events would happen around me, and, it sometimes felt, without me. I could be in the middle of a group, laughing and enjoying the joke of the moment, perhaps ad-libbing something in response, only to realize I wasn't heard. By anyone.

During my junior year abroad in France, at the ripe old age of eighteen, I was in Paris for Christmas, and so excited that a friend, a secret crush really, was visiting from his junior year abroad in England.

I remember meeting him early one morning at a train station when he arrived. We immediately went to a nearby cafe to grab breakfast, because that's what you do when you're young and in Paris. I don't remember what we ate, although I can bet my plate contained a Pain Au Chocolat. As we talked and caught each other up on various happenings in our lives, I, perhaps emboldened by the delicious French pastry on my plate, remember thinking, *This is silly! I like him. I should tell him!* Moments later, my heart pounding in my chest, I started what I'm sure was a clumsy, but sincere, admission of my feelings.

I don't recall my words, but I remember feeling brave for starting to put myself out there. And before I even finished my heartfelt admission, my heart still pounding in my chest, the object of my affection, acting very much as if he hadn't heard a word I said, nonchalantly asked if we would be walking or taking the metro to where we were staying with a gaggle of my newfound study-abroad friends. I think I paused, looking at him for any indication that he had heard a word I said or intuited even slightly what I was attempting to convey... and seeing no sign of recognition there, I smoothly answered that we'd be taking the metro there. At that moment, I briefly wondered if I had perhaps dreamt the whole thing. Maybe I hadn't said any of those words out loud? But in hindsight, what I was feeling wasn't unfamiliar. I had been here before. In the middle of the crowd, ad-libbing the joke, only to realize no one had heard a thing. I didn't have any kind of epiphany that day, nor for a long time after. I simply accepted and adapted to yet another situation.

But it started increasingly seeming to me that my adaptability, that trait that I had carried with such pride, was repeatedly betraying me. I found myself wondering, had I become so adaptable, that I had managed to completely become the chameleon, and in the process lost myself? When it came down to it, who was I really? Not the achiever, who graduated at fifteen. Not the young, serious intern, who was so intent on the spreadsheet she was assigned, that she ate lunch at her desk daily. Not the graduate student who was one of only two students selected by her peers to speak at graduate school commencement. Not the young consultant who aspired to and got each early promotion to which she set her mind. Was I the good daughter? The good sister? The good girlfriend? The good employee? Yes. All of these. And yet, not really.

Years later, as a young professional, I remember stopping dead in my tracks when, while reading an article in a business magazine, I came across the phrase *Imposter Syndrome* for the first time. I remember reading the passage several times, then thinking, *There's a NAME for that?* Wide-eyed, I turned to my boyfriend sharing the gist of the article only to hear him say, "Oh, I have that." My innate adaptability had long fed this belief that I was a fraud or imposter at work. That the "know-it-all" in me, who really didn't, would be caught out. The very successes and accomplishments others celebrated me for, I diminished in my own mind. This article, while reassuring in its assurance that this feeling was common (and unnecessary), also gave name to what I had experienced and thought for so long. Knowing I wasn't alone, and by all accounts, in good company, made it easier to understand, and ultimately dismiss this belief over time. It was hard work to truly accept that my accomplishments weren't all rooted in luck, or just being in the right place at the right time, or frankly, just a fluke, but that I, through my hard work and efforts, was central to each of them. Like so many of us, I had often dismissed and diminished my own efforts and took them for granted.

It was many years after this that I realized that, while I was at university and subsequently starting in the working world, I would often adapt in a particular way. Namely, I would take great pains to make sure I didn't appear to "know it all." I would soften my words and ask questioningly those things I knew as fact—always careful not to appear the smartest person in the room. At the time, I never linked my behavior back to those childish elementary school taunts of "know it all" that hadn't seemed to faze me at the time. And yet, those labels applied so early in life, *adaptable* and *know-it-all* were things I had unknowingly self-subscribed to and carried with me every day.

In practice, I reacted to each label differently. I became so adaptable over time that I struggled, for many years, believing I had no true sense of self. In contrast, I so firmly shunned the "know-it-all" that I often *played dumb* in situations I could have easily owned. And yet conversely, this also fed my belief that I was somehow supposed to know it all and would be showing weakness if I asked questions. It took concerted effort and years of work and life experience to break this last habit. To grant myself the freedom to not have all the answers—amazing! To start then asking the important questions—life-changing. And to begin being myself—liberating.

It took years for me to recognize that my adaptability—this thing I took for granted and once disavowed—is my core strength and so much a part of my success. It's what allows me to successfully course correct, pivot, and turn on a dime when my life, my work, or my family demand it to this day.

The realization that I came full circle in this journey still makes me smile. I look back on the pride I felt as a little girl when I marveled at the big word, even if I didn't know how it would shape my life. That little girl—I—somehow knew. In all those years where I had come to regard my adaptability as a short-coming or a deficit, I was fighting the truth. This persevering adaptability, a defining aspect of my personality, shaped me and my behaviors and ultimately made me the person I am today. The journey to this truth was perhaps a longer distance than I would have wished, but with it ultimately came the ability and willingness to accept myself. To me, there is no better journey's end.

And I love being able to say now: Yes, I'm still here: the adaptable girl; the versatile, successful professional; the flexible executive coach, trainer, and speaker. The ever-adaptable mom of five beautiful children. Whatever you want to call it, it's not some shadow that looms over me. Rather, this adaptability, this core ability to adapt—again, and again, and again—is something I now recognize as a strength, a differentiator, and a quality I own with pride. And to that little girl, I say, "Thank you for always believing in me."

Ati Rahbani Rexroad is a transformational coach, consultant, facilitator, and speaker. She and her husband are lucky parents, whose children teach them daily what adaptable truly means!

Beyond Coincidence

By Johannys Jiménez-Hartog

"And the day and the moment will arise and all of your pain and
fear and suffering will have vanished like a wind that pushes
the foam of the wave away, revealing the clarity of the ocean
beneath you…In your heart you will smile gently regardless of the
circumstances in which you find yourself."
— The Way of Mastery

It was like I was deaf when I was told the news. My brain couldn't
process what my ears had just heard.

The afternoon of that summer of June 2007 was bright and
beautiful. I was at home when the phone rang. It was the doctor's
office calling to give me the results of my breast biopsy. I had felt an
unusual lump on my left breast, so I had it checked out. I was not
worried because my doctor said that my breast was itching due to

fungus, which could be treated with a topical medicine. The itching stopped so I just forgot about it. Plus, no member of my family had ever suffered from any kind of cancer.

A medical assistant was calling. "We have the results of your breast biopsy. Please make an appointment and come to the office and discuss it with the doctor."

Confident that the diagnosis was negative and that this woman didn't have any important information to relay, I said, "Can't you just tell me?"

I remember her words clearly. "Unfortunately, you have cancer." Her tone was almost casual.

"WHAT?"

"Unfortunately, you have cancer," she repeated.

"CANCER?" I gasped, shocked. The world stopped for a moment. I remember my heart racing.

She replied, "Yes. Your physician has all the information. She will call you. Have a good day."

"WAIT! Hold on a second. I don't know anything about cancer, but I know there are sizes, stages, degrees, types, and so forth. Give me that information before you hang up!" I pleaded.

"Oh! OK. Let me get your file." Let me get your file? She just left me numb, with no words of connection or understanding of what had just happened to me. I wondered, with amazement, does this woman have any depth of feeling? Is she aware of the effect of her words? She is giving me a life-changing diagnosis—I have cancer, for God's sake!

When she came back on the line, she told me, "I have good news for you. Your cancer is very small; it is in Stage 1 and is not aggressive. You can contact your physician who will give you all the information about the removal of your breast, chemotherapy, and radiation. Have a good day." And she hung up.

Oh my God! I instantly knew this illness threatened my very being, turned my existence upside down, and raised thousands of life issues. What now?

I was able to reach my physician. She gave me the same information as basically as she could. She said I should delay any plans to get pregnant and take care of the cancer first. I asked dozens of questions, which she patiently answered. She then connected me with her secretary who told me that they had sent an email to my husband telling him the news.

Oh my God! Jack is going to know by email that I have cancer; I can't let that happen!

I called him, wanting him to hear this staggering diagnosis from me, but he didn't answer. Thirty minutes later, I called again. No answer. I texted him to call me.

Finally, Jack called. "Mi amor, I am on a break from a big meeting. ¿Qué pasa?"

"Well," I said in the most joyful and calm voice I could fake at that moment, "I spoke with the doctor and she said that I have a tiny, little, non-aggressive form of cancer."

"WHAT?"

"It's nothing to worry about. It's just something minor."

He saw through me and stammered that he would leave for home immediately.

Jack and I had been married for five years. We loved each other with all our hearts, enjoying a relationship that was close to perfect. I didn't want him to worry or to suffer. We had already surmounted the challenges of differences in age, religious/cultural backgrounds and language, and three miscarriages. Before I could continue with my thoughts, Jack was home. We were scared, crying, and hugging each other.

That evening I had to facilitate a service, *Prayers, Meditation, and Songs from the Heart*, at the Unity Church where I was training. Jack assured me I could cancel and stay home, but I felt I needed to do the service for my own sanity, to reconnect to the Self that existed before the life-changing phone call. I delivered my message and sang, just like every Wednesday, with passion, love, and joy from my heart.

At the end of every service, as always, I offered to pray with anyone seeking prayer support. A young woman approached me. "Can you please pray with me?"

"Sure," I said. We sat down and held hands. I lovingly looked at her sad eyes and asked, "What do you want prayer for?"

She paused, and then tearfully said to me, "What do you say to somebody that you love with all your heart who has just been diagnosed with cancer?"

WHAT? I was stunned. At that time, I was the director of the prayer group at the church. During the training, I always told the prayer trainees that whenever they are asked to pray for someone, they will find that they really will be praying for themselves because that's the way God has to communicate Presence.

I instantly knew that Divine Wisdom, Universe, Infinite Mystery, Sacred Space, that which we call God, had shown up to support me. But, with this specificity?

Working hard to maintain my composure, "Well…" I answered, not really knowing where the words were coming from. "Let your friend know how much you love her and care for her. Tell her that she is not alone, that God is present in her life right here and right now. And if she has a Spiritual Guide—"

"She believes that Jesus Christ is her Teacher and Spiritual Companion," she interrupted me.

The same as mine! "Then tell her that He will walk with her every step of this process. That she is not alone, and all is well." I knew God was talking through and to me.

Fortunately for me, my faith has been unwavering, enriched by wide-ranging spiritual studies. I was raised by loving parents who were deeply Catholic. The mystical teachings of this faith captivated me, and as a teenager led me to *A Course in Miracles*. By 2007, I was a licensed unity teacher, had started the journey of becoming an ordained unity minister, and studied and taught others *A Course in Miracles* for many years. From this background, I knew that the illness was not witnessing the truth of Who I Am and that I was born with all I needed to express the greatness of my inner being.

Though my faith was strong, I knew the diagnosis had profoundly affected me. I endured periodic dark moods and strength-sapping episodes. The diagnosis preoccupied my thoughts, radically changed my plans, and dramatically affected my whole world. However, I chose to focus on the positive, seeing my life continuing with Jack and with my ability to use this and other experiences to help others. When dark thoughts crowded in, I refocused on my unshakeable faith in God's goodness.

My surgery to remove the tumor was scheduled. Although my eternal Self knew better, my pragmatic, engineering, and mathematician mind allowed my ego to cause me to spend many restless nights reviewing my past life and wondering about the future. I had been unable to carry babies to term, and now I doubted motherhood would ever be in my future. My thoughts centered on my husband Jack's loving concern and our life together.

The night before the scheduled early morning lumpectomy, while taking a shower, I heard a soft though strong inner voice, which I had heard before. The words were unmistakable. "The nightmare is over."

The nightmare is over! Thank you, God! Thank you, beloved Jesus! My knees buckled at the awesomeness of this assurance. I couldn't help but kneel down and say again and again, "Thank you, God." That night I slept like a baby knowing that everything was already OK.

On September 13, which happened to be The World Day of Prayer, I had the tumor removed. After the procedure, the surgeon told me: "You are the happiest person that I have ever operated on. You were smiling during the whole procedure."

I knew, just knew, that this whole episode would serve only to make me a braver, healthier, and more trusting person.

A few days later, the pathology results showed that I had no cancer cells around the tumor. There were no signs the cancer had spread anywhere. I didn't need chemotherapy. There was a recommendation to undergo radiation for six weeks, which I refused. I knew I was healed.

Throughout this journey, I found I was surrounded by angels. Although I shared the diagnosis with very few people, including family, those few who knew prayed for my recovery. And my beloved husband gave boundless love; he was my constant companion and rock.

I am still healthy, and my marriage is as loving as ever. I have a thriving online Spanish Ministry, Unity Para Todos (Unity for Everyone), and I am a certified Canfield Trainer. I teach principles of success to all individuals and groups using the Jack Canfield Methodology and everything I have learned through countless transformative studies and as a Unity minister, professional engineer, math teacher, and professional singer/songwriter/actress.

My faith has taught me that all challenges can be overcome through courage and persistent belief in the power of love. Whatever your profound positive belief about yourself may be, just believe it, work it, trust it, and empower your deepest Self to manifest the greatness of your being. Be brave. You are never alone.

Johannys Jiménez-Hartog is an experienced, multi-talented, engaging, and inspirational bilingual (Spanish and English) speaker, author, and personality. A Jack Canfield Certified Trainer and ordained Unity Minister, she holds a Bachelor's degree in Industrial Engineering and a Master's in Education. Prior to these studies, Johannys acted and sang professionally, principally in Puerto Rico, including leading roles in telenovelas and her own TV show. She has recorded CDs with her own original songs. In 2010 she founded Unity Para Todos (Unity For Everyone), an online ministry (www.unityparatodos.org). She can be reached at johannyshartog@gmail.com.

Be
X
Do
=
Have

Self-Empowerment –
My Key to Success

By Tammy Gibson

"Only those who will risk going too far can
possibly find out how far one can go."
— T.S. Eliot

As a child, I was very shy and quiet, always staying in the background, not wanting to be front and center. I just did my own thing and kept out of everyone's way. However, in grade seven, at age thirteen, I experienced events that would change my life. During that year I was bullied by a girl in school. Her name was Alice. She had long black hair, a thin body and face, and long pointy fingernails. She would threaten to scratch my eyes out if I didn't do what she said. She ordered me not to talk to the other girls in our class, not to look at certain boys, to always say good things about her when we were around others, and pick up after her when she dropped things (on purpose) in the school hallway. Basically, I was bullied into being her *fake* friend because she had no real friends.

I was in a constant state of fear around her and would look for ways to avoid running into her at school. I didn't have the courage to stand up to her. I was afraid to complain to my parents or other friends about her because I didn't want to bring attention to myself or the situation. I thought if I could ignore it maybe it would go away. That approach didn't change anything. By the end of the school year, I was feeling very stressed and out of control over the situation. I had gained weight (due to stress-induced eating) and did not feel good about myself.

One day, during outdoor recess at school, Alice found me by the merry-go-round, which was around the corner from the main school doors. I was talking to a few of my classmates.

"What are you doing?" she said. "I warned you not to talk to those girls." She started toward me, her eyes glaring, and her hands extended with those pointy talons drawing closer. Something inside of me then snapped. I'd had enough! Somehow, out of my mouth came the words, "NO, BACK OFF!" Alice continued toward me and the next thing I knew we were in an all-out girls' fight, rolling around on the ground, pulling each other's hair, yelling and screaming. When I think back on it now, it must have been quite a scene. One of the teachers finally heard the commotion and broke us up, and then escorted us to the principal's office. We each told our side of the story, separately, in Mr. Weston's office. I remember Alice coming out of his office, looking at me with this defeated, yet oddly enough, relieved look on her face. She slowly walked away down the hallway. From that day forward, Alice never bothered me again, and in fact, over the years we became friends.

I learned a powerful lesson that day. I realized if I wanted things to change, I was the one that needed to take action, no one else. I felt different—confident and brave. I now knew that I had the power within me to make change happen. The experience that day was one of the most empowering moments in my life. It raised my level of self-awareness and self-confidence, and would serve me well throughout my life.

Fast track to my graduation year. All graduates had to pick a quote of our choice to put under our graduation picture in the school yearbook. I was drawn to one particular quote by TS Eliot, "Only those who will risk going too far can possibly find out how far one can go." At the tender age of seventeen, I had no idea what a profound impact those few words would have on the rest of my life!

My first real job after graduating from university with a science degree was working for a pulp and paper mill about sixty miles from my hometown. I was an environmental technician, responsible for monitoring and testing air and liquid waste emissions. There I was, a young twenty-one-year-old female in my blue jeans, hard hat, and steel-toed boots, making the rounds of the pulp mill every morning. Not only was I the lone female among hundreds of males in the pulp mill, but I was also in the highest-paid union position. During the late seventies/early eighties there were not too many women in male-dominated roles like this.

It was obvious many of the men resented me because of my position and pay scale. Their attitudes and snide remarks created tension I was all too familiar with. Some would just ignore me, some would make rude comments, while others would outright flirt with me. Memories of the harassment and bullying I endured in my younger years came flooding into my head. I could have easily given in to the pressure and quit, but I remembered my lesson of self-empowerment all those years ago, and the T.S. Eliot quote I had selected for my yearbook. Those words were a powerful reminder of courage in my younger years. So much so, I had printed the quote out and tacked it on my office cubicle bulletin board for daily encouragement. I reminded myself that I had been hired over others based on my skills and knowledge to do a job and that's what I needed to do. I always treated my colleagues the same, trusted in myself and my abilities, and did the job at hand. Over time, I was accepted as an equal, and the working relationships greatly improved. But I knew, in the long run, this job wasn't for me. It was time to start taking more risks, to go further. After three years, I set a goal to work one more year and save $15,000.00, then quit and head to the big city.

A year later, at the age of twenty-five, I packed up a U-Haul and headed south 500 miles to the city. My parents were absolutely mortified that I had quit a well-paying job and was leaving home. I had no job, nowhere to live, just my belongings and my savings. Being resourceful, I soon found a place to live and a part-time job. My journey was all about taking responsibility for my life, setting goals, and taking action. If I wanted to succeed, I knew it was on me to make it happen.

Eventually, I landed a part-time position in a government health-related position. My ultimate goal was to get a full-time job with the government environment department, but this was a foot in the door. I had learned not to hold out for the ideal, but to take advantage of small opportunities as they came to me, each one moving me forward. Be patient, be persistent, and persevere. The three Ps I lived by then and still do today.

Every week I would drive by the environment department office building and tell myself, "I'm going to be working there one day soon". I would visualize myself driving into the parking lot, parking the car, and entering the building. I don't remember where I learned about visualization, I just knew that it worked for me. After three interviews my persistence paid off and I was offered a full-time position as an environment officer. By taking the necessary actions I achieved the outcome I wanted!

Interestingly, I was again the only female in a male-dominated field. In fact, I was the first female environment officer ever hired by the government. My new office cubicle was next to a loud, overbearing male. He quickly dubbed me, "the token one," referring to the government's mandate to hire more women in male-dominated fields, implying I was hired for this position because I am a woman and not for my skill set. Once again, I was being put in a position to stand up for myself and what I had worked so hard to achieve. The T.S. Eliot quote was pinned to my office bulletin board. In fact, it was pinned in every office of every job I ever held. It was a constant reminder for me to continue taking risks and to grow as a person. I had become very proficient over the years in dealing with difficult people and now put those skills to work. I embraced the new nickname which took away any power this person thought he had over me. The daily teasing slowly dissipated, and I earned the respect of the other environment officers as a qualified colleague. Once again, I had empowered myself and gained confidence. I knew that I could take more risks toward even more success in my career.

I now set my sights on executive management, continuing to look for opportunities to get ahead. When I learned about a problem that the department executive was dealing with, I proposed a solution that included me playing a lead role. I essentially created new positions for myself with increasing levels of responsibility each time. My proposals were convincing and, to my advantage, no one else was stepping up to the plate with other suggestions.

Over the next twenty years, I progressed in my government career from a front-line worker to an executive director in upper management. All of these advancements were appointed positions because I provided a solution to a problem. I don't say this to brag, but rather to show how being proactive, taking action, and asking for what you want can bring you the outcomes you want. I followed my internal drive to continually set goals and take action. It wasn't always easy and at times I was faced with my male colleagues telling me I was too aggressive, too direct. However, I believed in myself and trusted my management approach, always looked for ways to support my team and empower them to be their best. When their job performance improved, that would only reflect positively on me.

The challenges and experiences over my life have taught me many things, but most importantly that I always had what I needed to succeed. In fact, we all do. We just have to be bold enough to take some risks and forge ahead. Here are some principles I have used that have helped me do that:

- To believe in myself and my abilities. The road wasn't always easy and at times I doubted myself, but I always believed I had what it took to get what I wanted in my career and my life.

- To accept responsibility for things that happened in my life. I knew I had the power within me to change things if they weren't going the way I wanted.
- To always set goals, and then once I reached them, to set more goals, always stretching myself further.
- To take action on my goals to get the results I wanted.
- To always ask, ask, ask! Ask questions and learn. Ask for what I want.
- To share what I learned with others, to help them empower themselves as well.

I hope what I have shared here will help you in some way to become more self-empowered and live the life you have always dreamed of. It's in you to do and yours for the taking!

Tammy Gibson is a retired public servant in executive leadership and a thirty-year competitive amateur golfer who has now turned her passion into a career as a Golf Success Coach. She and her golf-pro husband Barry own a joint business called Hole In One Success. Their mission is to inspire and motivate golfers and other athletes to feel better, move better, and be better, on and off the golf course. Tammy is a certified block therapist, certified Jack Canfield Success Principles Trainer, and is Titleist Performance Institute (TPI) certified for golf fitness. Tammy combines her training, coaching, and golf background with success principles to get the best results for her clients. You can reach her at info@ holeinonesuccess. Her website is: www.holeinonesuccess.com.

A Child's Vivid Imagination Saved My Career—and My Life

By Shannon Faulkner

"Visualization is the human being's vehicle to the future – good,
bad or indifferent. It's strictly in our control."
— Earl Nightingale

"Now, how did this happen to me again? Here again?" I asked myself.
Well, looks like yet another challenging situation to overcome.
I'm standing in the middle of my hostel room in Uluru, Australia (Ayers
Rock), and my sleeping bag has disappeared. Well, disappeared by the
five-finger magic trick I assume. I'm not sure why anyone would want
the smelly bag that I had been sleeping in for the past five months. It
had so much duct tape around the rips it might have been mistaken
for a silver parachute. Nevertheless, it's gone.

"Think, Shannon! Think!" In the next few hours, the sun will disappear. There are no outdoor stores nearby. When the temperature drops below freezing, it won't be much warmer in this hostel with no central heating. I quickly check my paper greyhound coach schedule (well, it is 1995) and see that there is a bus coming through this small town in the next hour. I pack what little gear I have into my rucksack, head to the front desk to check out, and off I go on my next adventure—on to Melbourne.

When I told my mother about that night, she was neither amused nor troubled. "Mum, something really awful could have happened out there."

"Yes, dear," she said. "But you found your *special* glasses, didn't you?"

We both smiled.

My mom likes to tell me a story from when I was five. She tells me that she would look at me thinking, "How does this little girl of mine always know where she wants to go?" She would tell me to trust my magic "vision glasses." When I put these on, I imagined that I could see the path ahead of me with such clarity and detail. These vivid pictures in my head created such an excitement for adventure—and a confidence that was beyond explanation.

When I was only six, I found an old plastic paddling pool with Smurf pictures all over it. I convinced my friends that when I go to the other side of the slue (a creek full of sewer sludge), a local newspaper would write about me. I didn't get a headline in the paper, but I did make it across the cesspool and back without falling.

One successful adventure after another gave me greater confidence, and energy to try new things. Crazier things. I had so much fun as a carefree child. I can't tell you how many times people would say,

"Shannon, I'm exhausted hearing about what you do every day. I can't imagine even trying to do any of these things."

This continued into early adulthood. I was wearing my glasses when I had the vision of standing in my cap and gown, with my smiling family around me, after graduating from college. I would be the first one on my dad's side to get a college education. Heck, I was the second person in my family to graduate high school—the first was my older brother! My parents didn't have the knowledge, education, or finances to help me get into college, so this really was a big stretch goal.

I had a vision, so it had to become reality. I sought the knowledge on my own, but the answers were not in textbooks. Visualization created opportunity for me. I remember the moment, at age seventeen, when two of my high-school friends from our small logging town of Squamish, BC Canada, asked if I wanted to come on their fourteen-hour road trip to Edmonton, Alberta, to check out a college. "Of course!" I said. Five years later, I was on that podium wearing my gown, locking eyes with my smiling family in the audience as I received my diploma from THAT graduate school! I felt as if this could only have been achieved through visualization and goal setting.

At first, my imaginary vision glasses gave me the confidence to try new things. As time went on, I realized that the glasses may have been imaginary, but the power of my vision was real. When I have a vision of something, it just seems to come true. I trust it and I make it happen. And then that stopped.

As an adult, something changed. I can't tell you the day I took my vision glasses off. But somewhere along the way, I stopped trusting my vision and I put on everyone else's glasses. I found myself living the life I thought they wanted me to live. That's when life got hard. Really, really hard.

Fast forward to 2010, I am standing in a room. It's not a hostel this time. I'm in my three-bedroom house in London, England. I'm looking in the mirror, and I don't see me. I see someone who is now twenty pounds overweight after experiencing yet another miscarriage, spending Friday evenings drinking red wine on my own in front of the TV, thankfully blessed with two amazing sons asleep upstairs. I also see that I'm in a very unhappy marriage, and am commuting five hours a day to a career job that ceased to be fulfilling years before. "What happened?" I asked myself. "When did my free-spirited life of traveling the world, educating myself on everything and anything from Japanese to Samba classes stop, and this life, what I deem to be 'white picket fence', begin? Was it when I had my first child, or when I got married, or when I decided to climb the corporate ladder so that I could own all this stuff surrounding and suffocating me now? Or was it others' expectations of what I should do? Is it the vision of others I have been following? To get married, buy a house, have a stable career, and have kids?"

I wasn't sure. What I did know is that I needed to do something to find out how I got here and find something quick. So, I did what I believed was the best plan of action: I bought a bicycle.

Have you ever been on a bike, the wind blowing through your hair and whistling in your ears, as you throw yourself down the hill at a speed that probably shouldn't be achieved by a parent of two young ones who depend on you to still be there to tuck them into bed? Well, if you haven't achieved this, or it's been a while and you are physically able to, I encourage you to get back on a bike. It was at this moment that I found in my pocket my old, but still usable vision glasses. When I cleaned them up with the tears from my sleeve and put them back on, I started to rediscover the ability to set goals again. The vision wasn't clear initially, but as the miles passed under my tires I felt that I could see where and how I lost my vision for my life.

Riding my bike allowed me the freedom to get out and rediscover me. I signed up for every charity race event and long-distance challenges. One of these was riding the 964 miles across Britain in nine days, which gave me the most clarity of vision for my life ahead, and I pivoted from there. I knew what I needed to do again: Create vision goals for the person I want to be, where I want to be, and how to achieve this. I needed to begin taking responsibility for all of life's challenges, past, present, and future. It wasn't going to be easy. I knew I would disappoint others, people would fear the change in me, my decisions would not always be right for them, thus risking being misunderstood. I would lose people I loved along the way, this I knew, but the most important person I would gain was me.

Four years later, I left my secure corporate job and set up my own successful management consulting company, my now ex-husband and I decided it was best to separate, my beautiful amazing boys live with me, and I have educated myself on developing my business and self-development, not with one course but five—three at the same time! I also lost all of the excess weight! Having a vision and setting goals has allowed me to give back to others through donating time and money, as a member of many leadership forums such as those empowering women. I am now reliant on myself for creating my own wealth. Only through finding my vision and setting goals to achieve my best life could I have achieved these.

So, what are my goals for the future now that I have my vision again? Well, it is very clear to me, as I feel the warm breeze upon my face looking out across the Puerto Rican bay, sitting beside my new husband in our rattan chairs on the veranda. We have our laptops out, planning our next global speaking trip to help others form their life vision.

Now I ask you, where will your vision glasses take you?

If you don't have vision glasses, ask yourself what childhood belief, story, or dream do you need to revisit and incorporate into your life so you can regain the happiness you seek.

Shannon Faulkner is an operational turnaround consultant in financial services, as well as, author, coach, mentor, and speaker. Using her collaborative hands-on approach and coaching skills, she enhances her clients' experience of what success means for them. This allows her clients to achieve their aspirations for their business and achieve their vision no matter how large or small they may be. To reach out to Shannon you can contact her through her company, Management Coaching Ltd. at hello@managementcoaching4u.com.

When the Student is Ready, the Teachers Appear

By Paula Harris

"The indispensable first step to getting the things you want out of life is this: decide what you want."
— Ben Stein

My life and career had been on an upward trajectory. At twenty-six I bought a home on my own. At twenty-eight I married my high school sweetheart, Bill, after dating for eleven years. As he joked, we were in the getting-to-know-you phase for a long time. In my mid-thirties, after a career in campus recruiting and human resources at consulting and financial services firms, I began working with Bill in our own registered investment advisory firm. By my late thirties, I held my first board presidency of a regional symphony orchestra and, soon after that, I held the chairmanship role of a 1400-member chamber of commerce. Life was good. Mostly.

Since college, I had slowly put on weight. However, I didn't feel my weight was holding me back from living my life, even when my doctor told me I was, "morbidly overweight," when I was forty. I had thought I was active enough by playing golf and practicing yoga.

I was now almost forty-seven years old. I was 5'2' and had reached a peak weight of 235 lbs. I knew that was not skinny, but I didn't feel I was morbidly overweight. In my mind, that label was usually reserved for people who weighed 300 or 400 pounds and binged on bags or boxes of food at a single sitting. Surely that was not me! I would see my face in the bathroom mirror every day, but rarely would I look in a full-length mirror or at photos of myself. I didn't allow myself to truly *see* myself until that December of 2013 when Bill and I attended Tony Robbins' *Date With Destiny*.

I had been to plenty of conferences before but *Date With Destiny* was nothing like I had ever experienced! It was like attending a rock concert where you dance, yell and sing, give and get hugs as well as shoulder massages. It was electrifying! I felt charged with positive energy!

I had envisioned myself winning something at the event and sure enough, on day two, Tony Robbins called out my name and I ended up on stage with Tony himself. I was in front of 2,500 people dancing and playing full out as I got to spin The Wheel! When Tony asked me what I wanted to win I shouted out, *Life Mastery* Rather, I won a free ticket to *Unleash the Power Within* in Dallas later that year—a four-day program. Still a great prize! Little did I know that was just the beginning of my winning, learning, and growing that week.

Before I go further, I need to confess that I had only heard of Tony Robbins—I knew he wrote books, did infomercials and my husband had a set of tape cassettes that he would listen to in the car, but that was the extent of my knowledge. Also, personal development was not something I had really delved into, other than some workshop at Kripalu, a yoga retreat center in western Massachusetts. I had not been someone who set goals, did visualizations and affirmations. But my life was about to change.

Amazing things happened to me as a result of being on stage with Tony and playing full out. First, it allowed me to connect with so many people in the audience. All week-long people were introducing themselves to me because I had been my authentic self on stage which allowed for genuine connections. On day three, I came back to my seat to find a woman from Robbins' exclusive Platinum Partners group waiting for me. She shared that one of "The Plats" saw me on stage and noticed I didn't win what I asked for and he wanted to anonymously gift *Life & Wealth Mastery* to me—a nine-day program. I was floored that anyone would do something like that for me. I was being taught the lesson of gratefully receiving, as I was the one normally giving to others.

There was so much learning that week. We learned about limiting beliefs—roadblocks that prevent our development and growth, we learned about moving towards and moving away from values, we set goals, created visualizations and affirmations to assist with our successful accomplishment of those goals. But the real eye-opener for me was when I watched the video of myself on stage and truly *saw* myself and how large I really was. I knew at that moment I needed to change. I set the goal to live to be 114 and, in order to achieve that goal, I needed to get healthy. I needed to lose weight. I wanted to shed 100 pounds over the next eighteen months.

With a breakthrough goal such as this, I needed to find the resources to help me get there. One was the gift of the *Life & Wealth*

Mastery Program where I would spend the first four and a half days learning about nutrition, healthy choices and lifestyles as well as participating in a food cleanse. But I needed to start right now, today. And then I remembered the first person I met when I arrived at *Date With Destiny*—Johnny. He was a chiropractor in California but used to live in Massachusetts. When I told him I lived in Duxbury, MA, he told me to make an appointment with Dr. Katina Manning, a fellow chiropractor, who would change my life—even if there was nothing wrong with me. He said she had helped him change his life.

On December 23, 2013, I had my first appointment with Dr. Manning. I shared with her my goals, especially my breakthrough goal of shedding 100 pounds and she poked me gently in the arm.

She said, "Lose weight? You won't be able to lose weight until you stop inflaming yourself."

Initially, I had no idea what that meant and soon came to understand that when you are eating foods that don't agree with your body, your body goes into a state of fight. My body was trying to protect me from harm and was not in a state of ease to release weight. I'm sure it's more technical than that but that's how I understood it. I took a Food Inflammation Test (FIT) to find out what foods inflamed my body because everybody is different. Next, I went on a thirty-day food cleanse and basically ate a Whole 30 diet, which is a food plan where you remove all of the potentially inflammatory foods and beverages in your diet and eat clean for thirty days.

During all this, she continued to adjust me so that my internal organs and body worked optimally and I began to release weight. I kept up with my yoga practice and felt my body move with less pain and more ease.

I'm so grateful for the resources I received to help me better understand my weight issue and develop a solid plan to achieve my goals. I am grateful for Johnny urging me to see Dr. Katina and for my own innate wisdom to act to make that appointment. Dr. Katina continues to be a consistent part of my health and wellness routine, as is my Fitbit that I now wear daily to ensure I get my 10,000 steps, a good night's sleep, and drink half my body weight in ounces of water each day.

In 2015, I made it to 70% of my weight loss goal, then plateaued and have crept up a bit. It's now time to take action again. I have reset my breakthrough goal to shed weight again. For me, it's less about what the number on the scale is and more about moving my body with ease. In honestly evaluating my food choices, I am more disciplined than I have ever been and am making decisions to cut out certain food categories. It's much easier to cut out a food category than to have to make a decision every time you are faced with that food choice. I have taken the FIT test again to see what my inflamers are now and met with a holistic nutritionist.

I have developed a vision and some affirmations that have been written in a way to support me in achieving these next-level goals in my life. Having a healthy body will provide me with more certainty to achieve them.

Constant and never-ending improvement is now a daily focus for me. I've learned that I can decide what I want in this life and live deliberately towards those goals. Rarely does one achieve their goals without enlisting the help of others, so I am better at asking for what I need and want. I have surrounded myself with a team of coaches for life, business, and health, as well as accountability partners and mastermind groups. This vast team of people helps guide me forward so that I can be the best version of myself.

Paula Harris is part-financial-advisor and part-dream-architect, who takes great pride in helping her clients, particularly widowed women, obtain financial peace of mind while they get back on their feet, rise up and navigate their path forward. Paula is an engaging speaker and leader with deep community roots. She enjoys assisting people in the life planning that goes hand-in-hand with financial planning and is the creator of Rise Up Success Training and Retreats. She can be reached at www.whcornerstone.com.

Retirement to Rewirement

By George Brown

"Retiring just so you can do nothing is no way to live and
so from now on, the word retirement will be
replaced with the word 'Graduation.'"
— Mike Finley

I'm a successful guy. I have been married to my wonderful wife, Susan, since 1982. I have two loving daughters and two fun grandkids. I'm the chief engineer in a leading company. I'm at the top of my career. At sixty-two, my life is on cruise control. That is about to change.

I was at work one day, having coffee with one of our contractors. "George," he says. "When are you planning to retire?"

I mentally pushed on the brakes. I was no longer on cruise control. I didn't know what to say. It felt like I was staring at an iceberg in front of me. My mind was blank except for deny, deny, deny. I spat out, "I'm never going to retire!"

When I got home from work, I began talking about it with Susan. I had a cold feeling in my chest. With this iceberg in front of me, I didn't know how to move forward toward retirement. Susan and I talked about it a lot. We went online and found an app for counting down to retirement. You put in your retirement date. You plug in all your vacation time, weekends, all your holidays, and any other time owed, and it tells you how many more working days till your retirement. Okay, so I had just over 500 working days until I retired at age sixty-five. Each day I wrote the number on a whiteboard in the kitchen on my way to work. This made it fun for a while. It gave me the feeling that I had everything under control. However, there was still a fear inside that I couldn't seem to calm.

To help take my mind off this, Susan suggested we go to a Jack Canfield event. She had always wanted to do that, ever since we listened to his material about high self-esteem on cassette tapes. I told her to go. Susan said, no. She wanted us to do this together. That's when I realized I needed to sit down with her and really listen to what she was suggesting.

We both signed up to attend *Breakthrough to Success* (BTS) in August of 2016. We got copies of his book, *The Success Principles*, and started reading it. Little did we know how this would change our lives.

On the first day at BTS, Jack taught that success begins with you taking more responsibility for your outcomes in life. By acting as if you are 100 percent responsible for your life you will have more success. I naively thought I'd got that responsibility part already, Jack. He then said, "You are responsible for your behavior (what you say and how you say it). You are responsible for your thoughts (self-talk) and your beliefs (both conscious and subconscious). You are responsible for your visual imagery (including your images for your future)."

It got me thinking about my future, once I retired. What future? All I saw was an iceberg.

I became engaged in the process, and during an exercise on increasing responsibility in one area of my life, I decided to take five percent more responsibility for my health by taking the stairs instead of the elevator at work.

At lunchtime, Kathleen Seeley, one of Jack's instructors, presented on how to explore this concept further. She said that when we experience an event, we make up a story in our head about the outcome of the event based on past experiences, and then respond with that story. The brain is extremely efficient at this. We often don't even realize we are doing it.

It reminded me of when I couldn't find the keys to my truck. I always leave them on the front lobby windowsill. I thought my wife must have used the truck and didn't put the keys back where I expected them to be. I was ready to get into it with her when I remembered that the day before I'd worn that yellow jacket because it was windy and got distracted by a phone call when I got home. Sure enough, there were my keys in the pocket of the jacket in the closet. That story I told myself about her having the keys had the potential to cause all kinds of trouble!

I was very interested in this lunchtime presentation. Immediately, I took a pen and drew a huge plus sign on a blank page in my notebook, as Kathleen has done on stage. Without hesitation, I wrote RETIREMENT in the top left quadrant of the page. That was the event I was facing. In the top-right quadrant, I wrote ICEBERG. This was the story I told myself about retirement. I felt blocked. In the bottom right quadrant, I wrote NEGATIVE/DENIAL/FEAR, which was my response. And finally, in the bottom left quadrant was my outcome where I wrote NONE. What wasn't I understanding? This hadn't helped. I put my hand up and asked, "What do you do if your outcome is not something you want?"

Kathleen said, "Look at your story and ask: Is it true? If you want a better outcome change the story you tell yourself. That will in turn change your response, leading to the outcome you want." What a concept!

I looked at my story and thought, could retirement be positive? I crossed out ICEBERG and wrote POSITIVE as the story I wanted to tell myself about retirement. Amazingly this calmed me down, and I considered possible outcomes and writing them all around a crossed-out NONE. I looked back and wrote in POSITIVE for my response to retirement instead of negative, denial, and fear. Ah, I was getting this! I was responding this time based upon a positive story I was telling myself, instead of reacting to a negative, false story. I now had all these positive ideas of what I could do once I retired.

I felt really good. I still had to decide what I wanted, but now I had so many areas to explore. I could learn to play the piano. I would have more time with Susan and the kids and grandkids. I could work for myself. A new direction of my choice! Sure, I had to change how I thought about things. I needed to wire new pathways in my brain and forge new habits. I was excited! I had hope again.

I took one more look at the page and I saw that word RETIREMENT. I still didn't like that word. I didn't want it on the page. It didn't fit with the direction I was going. This wasn't stopping or an ending. It was a new beginning. A new direction. I just needed to think differently.

At the start of my story, I said that I was never going to retire. My next step was to reframe my event. I have now made the new event REWIREMENT, and it has such an interesting positive outcome. I'm so looking forward to what the future has in store for me now!

George Brown is from Calgary, Alberta, Canada, and is a first class power/stationary engineer. He worked in that field for forty-five years, taught power engineering at college for five years, and spent a winter working as a ski instructor. He has a BA from the University of Western Ontario. George is a Jack Canfield Success Principles transformational trainer and a Cultural transformational trainer certified consultant. He's been married for thirty-eight years to Susan and together raised two girls and now has two grandchildren. Retirement caused a crisis in his life and the success principles helped him work through it. He found the principles so useful he wanted to share his story to encourage anyone to seek out and adopt them in their life. Contact George at yourrewirementforsuccess@gmail.com.

THE COIN

By Nelly Torras

"We come this way but once. We can either tiptoe through
life and hope that we get to death without being too badly
bruised or we can live a full, complete life achieving
our goals and realizing our wildest dreams."
— Bob Proctor

Why do we settle for the safe and predictable way through life? That was certainly true of me. In 2018, I was working full-time as an economist for a successful consulting company in Europe. It was not an ideal place to work, but I was quite comfortable.

In my birthday month—August—destiny acted for me. A big investor bought the entire company. The buy-out forced me to reassess the path my life was taking. I realized I was not using all my personal strengths in my job. I love supporting people, giving feedback, and team building. I love dealing with leaders rather than bosses. I love collaboration instead of competition. I enjoy being part of a team. But I was tired of doing the same job over and over again without evolving. I was tired of working for others, not for me. Something inside told me that I deserved better. I wanted to feel the joy of doing a job that I loved. I wanted to grow and blossom as a professional and as a person.

But I did not dare make a change. I was divorced, and I was dedicated to the emotional needs of my twelve-year-old daughter. Also, I needed financial security. The idea of looking for a new job was overwhelming. The thought of working for another company—or even working on my own—doing exactly the same thing did not fill me with much enthusiasm. But I am not one to quit easily. So, initially, resistance and fear won. I waited and waited, until it was obvious that my time at the company was over. Regardless of the circumstances—my age, my marital status, my responsibilities as a parent—my life was changing whether I liked it or not.

This time was different, and I knew it.

I decided to give myself three months to identify my next career step. Working as a freelance economist, I had a few clients. Some job offers came my way. Headhunters called to see if I was interested in the jobs they were offering. I refused these offers. Then I was interviewed by a very important corporation, and they gave me new perspectives to consider. It was a tempting opportunity to have a very good position in a great company with a high salary. Instead of taking it, I let the offer go and decided to become more receptive to new events happening in my life.

I bumped into an old book called *The Secret* and began reading some chapters randomly. The book talked about The Law of Attraction. It states that if you focus on the positive things in your life, you will automatically attract more positive things into your life. But if you are focused upon negativity, then you will attract more negativity. On Netflix, I watched the movie adapted from the book. It featured Jack Canfield. Suddenly, I found that I was drawn into his message, and it really resonated with me. His ideas inspired me to take control of my life by confronting fear. He spoke about the importance of taking action and being 100% responsible for the results. He talked about the importance of understanding my inner self in order to identify my purpose in life. From Jack Canfield, I realized I had to believe in myself if I really wanted to succeed. Then I had to share the journey and make a difference in the world.

Although English is a second language for me, I became very committed to the American way of doing things. I joined new groups and had new conversations. I adopted an American schedule to more directly follow up posts and others' opinions. I was definitely engaged. Even though my English was a little rusty, I still was able to enjoy all I found on the way. I felt like a teenager being in a new Facebook group, with people helping each other and sharing our life adventures. My goal was to gain some practical resources and advice to enhance my own personal development.

At the end of 2018, I learned about one of Jack Canfield's online programs. Should I sign up? To be honest, it was one of my most difficult recent decisions. You may ask, "Why so difficult?" Quite simply, it was because I live in another country, on another continent, speak a different language and have a twelve-year-old daughter to take care of. It's as simple as that. But the decision went beyond just taking a course. There was something bigger. I am a grounded person, and I have been working on my personal development for years. But I was really scared about pursuing such a massive change in my life path after more than twenty-five years working in the financial sector.

Every day I thought about what should I do. I knew I wanted a change. No one could tell me what the future held. People could give me advice, but no one could make the decision for me. I alone was responsible. In other words, taking 100% responsibility for your life and the results of your actions.

The uncertainty made me so terrified. Decision day was approaching. It was at that extreme moment when I remembered that someone had told me to test myself by tossing a coin. I took an English fifty pence coin in my hand and got ready to flip it—heads or tails. I was shaking with fear and full of turmoil. Heads meant *Do the course* and all it involved. Tails meant *No, don't go*. The coin flipped in the air and landed. Tails.

Looking at that coin, I remembered The Law of Attraction. The coin had picked up on my inner vibrations and reflected my inner self-doubt and fear. That's why it landed on *tails*. Looking at that coin, I was able to realize what I really wanted. So, I picked up the coin again. Feeling aligned with my purpose in every cell of my body, I tossed it in the air again. This time it was *heads*. I tossed it, again and again, on and on, and it always landed on *heads*. Awesome. The coin itself was not important. It simply showed me the truth. I wanted to take action and enroll in the course. Once I made the decision, I became calm and relaxed. The turmoil was gone.

What you want lies on the other side of fear. I had learned the lesson. You need to feel the fear and take action anyway.

Since then, everything I have done has been very enriching—full of adventure, sacrifice, trust, and belief. In fact, it's been a journey full of knowledge in every sense, as I am working hard to take a new career path, to empower people to achieve their goals, giving them the support and help they need to fulfill their professional and personal wishes.

My knowledge as an economist has merged with the new—inspiring, guiding, and supporting other people. This is my passion. I am on my own, doing what I want and this makes me feel good and alive. I continue to move along my chosen path to become the person that I want to be, serving the community with my head and my heart, doing what fulfills me, inspiring, teaching, guiding, sharing—and always learning.

Sometimes we find ourselves at a point of no return. There is something that really scares us, but we have to move on anyway. You cannot look back. The story of Lot's wife from Genesis 19 comes to mind. When Lot and his family were escaping from Sodom and Gomorrah, they were instructed not to look back to the land they had left. But his wife did and immediately turned into a column of salt.

This is only an example, but it reminds us that going forward always takes us somewhere. Looking back or standing still is not going to bring you what you really want. It's much better to take action.

This is the message: Experience your fear, take action anyway, and you will find many wonderful surprises that will make you feel full of love, both for yourself and for others.

For almost thirty years Nelly Torras has been an economist, specialized in auditing and advising diverse companies. Nelly has developed her coaching methodology over the last few years, consolidating a new path as a consultant, speaker, trainer, and coach. Nelly is dedicated to working with entrepreneurs, small business owners, and corporate executives providing them with the tools to achieve their goals. Nelly's clients receive the help and support to reach both professional and personal objectives. Nelly can be found at www.nellytorras.com.

You're Out of Order: Opportunity for Improvement

By Sherry McCool

"We all need people who give us feedback.
That's how we improve."
— Bill Gates

On a chilly, spring evening, I arrived early for a weekly meeting I attend with a group of ten or twelve women. As I walked in, the meeting chairperson asked if I would introduce a topic for discussion that night, since the person designated to do that was out of town. I agreed, found a chair, and happily noticed two newcomers.

The meeting began as usual with an invocation and meditation. Then it was time for the discussion portion of the meeting. Since I didn't have a prepared topic, I chose to ask if anyone in the group had something they wanted to discuss. I glanced around the table and there was no response.

At that moment, seeing the two newcomers, I recalled when I was new to the group and how welcomed I had felt when asked if there was something I wanted to discuss. With that recollection firmly in mind, I deviated from the usual protocol and asked one of our new participants if there was anything she wanted to discuss. She smiled and said there was not. As I spoke with the other newcomer, a long-time member of the group, someone I respected and admired, loudly interrupted me with a stern and agitated comment. "Sherry, you're out of order! That's not the way things are done here!"

I was genuinely taken aback. I knew I had strayed from the routine and technically, her statement was correct. Nevertheless, I decided I was not going to stop the meeting to explain my decision or rationalize my deviation from protocol. I smiled and nodded to acknowledge I had heard her comment. I then shifted my focus back to the newcomer with the intention to finish our interaction and move quickly to a topic.

However, to my surprise, the tenured member pushed back her chair, stood up, and in an angry tone said, "This is not how this meeting is supposed to be run. This is not 'The Sherry Show!' The chairperson should not allow you to do this. Sherry, you're always trying to be in charge, and that isn't what this meeting is about." And, she walked out.

I was stunned. Her angry outburst left me with what I'm sure was a deer-in-the-headlights look on my face. My heart now pounding in my chest, I thought to myself, "WOW! That was some emotionally charged, unexpected, negative feedback."

I observed the energy in the room had abruptly shifted from calm and peaceful to tense and uncomfortable. At that moment, a quick prayer flashed through me as I remembered several things I had learned. Heart still pounding, I suggested to the group that we pause, breathe, and sit quietly for a moment.

Then I shared a favorite learning and powerful concept that has consistently supported me throughout my life. Namely that when unsettling or unexpected events happen in life, each of us has a choice in how we respond. With that in mind, I suggested we start the meeting over with a simple prayer and proceed with the topic: How We Handle Life When Unexpected or Difficult Things Happen.

With the awkwardness of the earlier episode acknowledged, people felt comfortable talking about how they felt, shared meaningful personal stories, and we enjoyed a truly relevant and useful meeting.

I left the meeting that night truly grateful for the coaches and mentors I've had in my life. Because of my work with them, I had the tools to effectively handle an unexpected and difficult situation without getting angry, upset, retaliating, or having a meltdown. As I drove home, I also had a chance to reflect on the fact that no matter how it was delivered, I had been given important feedback, and it was up to me to decide how I was going to respond.

That night, before I turned off my phone for the night, I heard that small intrusive beep indicating I had email. Checking my inbox, I found an email from the outspoken meeting attendee. She wrote that although she regretted storming out of the meeting earlier, she did not regret anything she had said. She provided additional observations and closed with an offer to meet with me in person to discuss this further.

As I read her message, I found myself thinking of Ken Blanchard's words: "Feedback is the breakfast of champions." The next morning, I replied, thanking her for the relevant, specific, and timely feedback. I agreed to meet with her and we set up a meeting for a few days later at her home.

With our encounter fresh in my mind, and anticipating our upcoming meeting, I felt a sense of responsibility to prepare and pulled out a favorite book, *Nonviolent Communication* by Marshall B Rosenberg. Over the years, Marshall has been a go-to resource as I've read and reread that book, studied with him at the Omega Institute in New York, and even became certified as a mediator.

Reviewing my well-worn book, two things I had previously underlined stood out to me. The ideas of consciousness and communication.

- Consciousness: principles that support living a life of compassion, collaboration, courage, and authenticity. Understanding how words contribute to connection or distance.
- Communication: knowing how to ask for what I want, how to hear others, even in disagreement, and how to move toward solutions that work for all. Sharing "power with others" rather than using "power over others".

I realized I needed to come from a place of conscious communication and be honest without implying criticism.

In the days leading up to our meeting, I also made extra use of Hoʻoponopono, a clearing process of reconciliation and forgiveness learned from Dr. Joe Vitale and Dr. Ihaleakala Hew Len, co-authors of *Zero Limits*. Consciously repeating to myself, "I love you. I'm sorry. Please forgive me. Thank you." I became acutely aware of the importance of being 100% responsible for having created the situation and the need to resolve it by practicing love and forgiveness. When the day came for our meeting, I felt prepared to be fully present, to own my part, and listen with an authentic loving heart.

From my perspective, our meeting was a success and provided a breakthrough opportunity for us to get to know each other better. It was also helpful to learn that an interaction she and I had had years earlier—something I didn't even immediately recall—was a big part of her anger and frustration with me. Our time together allowed me to appreciate how she, as well as others, might experience me regardless of my motives, intentions, or assigned duties.

Toward the end of the meeting at her home, she asked if I'd ever been in management. I smiled and shared that I had worked for Marriott International for thirty-four years and had been in numerous management positions. However, I understood it was not my place to manage, supervise, or try to be the leader for our weekly women's meeting. I did my best to reassure that I valued the women's meeting and wanted to do my part to ensure it remained a healthy, vibrant, and welcoming meeting for everyone.

When our conversation ended, we hugged and I left feeling happy and grateful to have received her feedback with an open mind and a loving heart. I also knew I had work to do.

As Kathie Dannemiller, co-author of *Whole-Scale Change Toolkit* once told me, "Sherry, point your finger at yourself and say these words, 'If it's meant to be, it's up to me!'" I knew Kathy's message was as true now as it had been almost thirty years earlier.

It was up to me to do something with the feedback I had been given, and I'm glad to report I took action. Now, instead of saying yes to many of the requests I receive, I have found ways to defer them to others or to just say NO. Plus, I stepped down from several service positions and stopped allowing myself to be volunteered to handle conflict-prone situations. As I took action, I was relieved to find I was being accountable to myself at different levels, and new opportunities to be of service found their way to me! I had more time to travel and reconnect with people important to my values and purpose. Amazingly, I had less stress and experienced more peace because I was willing to take action on some unexpected negative feedback.

Once upon a time, such feedback frightened, overwhelmed, and intimidated me. I interpreted it as a failure and as a message that I wasn't good enough. Today, I'm grateful for feedback and see it as an improvement opportunity enabling me to reach my goals and make my dreams come true.

And the outspoken person from earlier in the story? I'm happy to report since our meeting and heartfelt talk, we have become real friends who enjoy spending time together and know we can count on each other in good times and tough times. WOW—the power of feedback!

Sherry McCool is the creator of Success Looks Great On You and the founder of McCool Consulting, LLC. Her goal is to help frustrated business leaders achieve breakthrough results and be successful in all areas of their lives. She believes everyone should have healthy, happy successful lives that bring them joy. Sherry successfully held numerous leadership positions during her thirty-four-year career with Marriott International, and she combines that experience with her expertise as a certified Canfield Trainer and a Barrett Values Model Practitioner to deliver transformational events. Visit www.successlooksgreatonyou.com to learn more or connect with Sherry at sherry@successlooksgreatonyou.com.

Touching a Billion Lives

By Sunil Parekh

"The two most important days in your life are the
day you are born and the day you find out why."
— Mark Twain

L ife was great. Everything seemed to be going exactly the way I
wanted. I was excelling in my academics, winning awards and gold
medals, studying in some of the premier institutions in India and the
USA, and I was getting a lot of love and respect from everybody! At
twenty-four, could anyone ask for anything more?

But on February 6, 1994, everything changed for me. It was a
normal Sunday morning. My family and I went for a long outing,
not expecting that this day would be the blackest day of my life. At
that time, there were no mobile phones and pagers in India, so there
was no way for anyone to contact me. When I returned home in the
evening, I saw there were lots of people waiting outside my house
wearing white clothes. This indicated that somebody had passed away

in my house. I was scared. Who could it be? Was it my grandfather? Or was it my grandmother? These were the questions that were racing in my mind. But when I entered my house, I saw that it was my father lying dead on the floor. I was only thirty at the time and my father was everything to me—not only emotionally, but he was also the backbone of my business, managing the finances of the company.

Everything started going wrong. There were lots of financial challenges in my business. At the end of the year, I found out that my business had suffered a huge loss of US $750,000. I was completely shaken up and did not know what to do. At that time, US $750,000 seemed to be more like $5 million today! It was like a huge mountain of debt in front of me.

I was frantically looking for solutions as I struggled through some of the darkest times in my life. But as they say, when the student is ready, the teacher appears. The same happened to me. I suddenly came across a book called *Silva Mind Control Method*, which taught me how to use my subconscious mind to solve problems in my life. I started applying what I had learned in the book and from related workshops and, to my surprise, I was able to completely solve my financial problems within two-and-a-half years. But the magnitude of these financial challenges led me to put an end to my entrepreneurial journey. I sold my business and joined the corporate world. I started applying the same techniques in my corporate job and then there was no looking back. I made it to the highest position of a COO in one of the leading animation studios in India. I made a lot of money, became very successful, was traveling around the world, had over 800 people working for me and life was beautiful once again.

However, in spite of the unimaginable success in the past ten years, I did not feel my life was complete. There seemed to be a big vacuum. That is when Jack Canfield, one of the world's leading transformational coaches, came into my life. Jack was visiting India in April 2012 and I attended one of his Success Principles workshop. Though this workshop was only four hours, there was one thing that struck me very hard, and that was the concept of understanding your life purpose. I understood that the unhappiness that was there in my life was because I had never understood the purpose of my life. In fact, I had never even understood what life purpose meant. After the workshop, I understood what it means to live a purposeful life. I immediately signed up for a personal coaching program and became very clear on my purpose. When I did some of the exercises and meditations in the program it became very clear that I was meant for teaching. When I had taught in the past, I would experience tremendous joy. I felt God had given me a very special quality which was to make very complex subjects easy. The second thing I noticed was that I loved helping people. I learned that the only way to find out whether you are ON PURPOSE or OFF PURPOSE is by the amount of JOY you experience in your life. I clearly discovered that by using my teaching skills I could inspire, motivate, and empower people to live happier and healthier lives.

Hence my purpose was discovered, which is: To inspire, motivate, and empower people to live happier, healthier, and more successful lives.

Once my purpose became clear, everything I did was in alignment with my purpose. There was no confusion. I was never confused about what I should do and what I should not do. My purpose stood like a lighthouse which always guided me to what I was supposed to do.

After understanding my purpose, the next thing was to decide exactly what I wanted to be, do, and have in my life. So, I started deeply reflecting on what was it that I truly wanted. One day in 2012, when in deep meditation, the number *one billion* suddenly popped out of my head. The message that I got from my inner self was that I have to transform the lives of one billion people by December 31, 2032. This then became the mission of my life.

I quit my high-profile corporate job and started conducting training programs and workshops to transform lives. My wife Jasmine and I started Rise Development Academy in India. We conducted programs for people from all walks of life—students, businessmen, corporate professionals, homemakers, professionals such as doctors, and lawyers, etcetera. I honed my skills by taking several short-term and long-term courses trying to understand what is the best way to bring about lasting change in people's lives. I took training in the Success Principles and started teaching these principles to my participants. I attracted some of the best people from across the planet. My vision was very clear: transforming one billion lives. When your vision is very clear and you keep holding this vision in your mind using all the tools such as visualizations and affirmations, combined with taking action, the Law of Attraction is bound to attract people, events, ideas, opportunities, situations, and circumstances that can move you towards your vision.

This is exactly what started happening. As I started working on my goals and applied the Success Principles, I started attracting the right people who were the top influencers of India. They helped me reach out to the masses. While all this was happening, I still did not know how I was going to reach one billion people. One day, while I was meditating, a clear voice from within said, "Sunil, you cannot do this alone. You need like-minded people who can help you to take this work forward."

Hence, I launched a Train the Trainer program, which combined all the modalities that I had learned from masters across the world and also from masters in India. We have now conducted eight Train the Trainer sessions and have 110 certified transformation coaches across India and abroad. Today, at any given point in time, there are 110 coaches reaching out to people and transforming their lives. I feel that conducting the Train the Trainer program was something that my inner GPS system told me. The inner GPS system (our subconscious mind) is infinitely intelligent and guides us on what steps we should be taking to achieve our vision.

As I started applying the Success Principles, everything started to fall into place. While the journey was not easy, positive things were happening. I have to thank my wife, Jasmine, as she was always very supportive of my journey. We never gave up. While other trainers in the market were struggling, my calendar was full for four to five months. As we moved forward, we noticed that there are many people in India who need this work badly but cannot afford to attend paid workshops. So the next question was: If I really want to reach one billion people in India and abroad we will definitely need to reach the underprivileged sections of the society, but how? That is when the idea of starting a foundation came about. This was again guided by my inner GPS system. We started a foundation that conducts mental wellness programs, goal achievement programs, and success principles programs for the underprivileged completely free.

Today, we are conducting programs for students in underprivileged schools, prison inmates, police, defense personnel, women in distress, orphanages, old age homes, and many other places which are really needing this transformational work. Our 110 coaches are doing an excellent job in reaching out to every nook and corner of India, training all sections of the society.

The journey has only begun. There is still a lot to do. But today I feel confident that I will be guided at the right time in the right manner to reach my goal of transforming one billion lives by 2032. My next goal is to start teaching this work on radio, TV, and social media, and to have my books, online programs, and home study programs ready in the next two years. I owe all of this success to the Success Principles I learned and put into practice. If I had not understood the purpose of my life nor the importance of being clear of what I wanted and how to access the inner GPS system, I don't think I would be in this position today. My schedule is full, I make decent amounts of money and I touch thousands of lives directly or indirectly every month. Doing this work gives me the ultimate satisfaction and fulfillment that I'm now living a life that is meaningful and purposeful and also allows me to unleash my highest potential.

Today, I am very clear about what I need to do when I get up in the morning. I see myself working till the last day of my life, standing on my two feet, doing what I'm supposed to do, and then passing on. But when I pass on, I will be very happy knowing that I lived my life fully and left a legacy behind me. I owe my deepest gratitude to those who changed my life and giving me all the tools, techniques, and strategies to make such a big difference to this planet.

I feel that all of us must make all efforts to discover our life purpose. Once you discover it, you will find that life is no longer the same. Something magical happens and there is no limit to the JOY you can experience. Also, deciding on what you want is very critical. This way you can live your life by design rather than by default. I feel these are the two principles of success that made the biggest difference in my life.

Sunil Parekh is an international success coach, a subconscious mind expert, human potential trainer, keynote speaker, and author. He holds a Master's Degree in Computer Engineering from Virginia Tech, USA. Sunil quit after twenty-five years in the IT industry, to follow his passion for teaching. In 2011 he started the Rise Development Academy (www.riseda.com) and conducts transformational programs for people from all walks of life. He is a certified Canfield Methodology Trainer, Heal Your Life workshop leader, NLP practitioner, clinical hypnotherapist, Silva Graduate, and EFT practitioner. Sunil has a mission of transforming a billion lives by December 31, 2032. You can reach him at sunil@riseda.com.

In Conclusion

We are thirty-six former strangers who spent a year going through a transformational training program. At the end of our final live week together, Bob mentioned we should all write a book about what we had learned. Angie suggested it might be easier if we all just wrote a chapter, and the idea for *Life Lessons in Success* was born.

Our journey together did not end after the training. We carried it on by writing this book together. Each of us wrote a chapter, and we took on various roles: editors, book assemblers, marketers, social media roles, project managers. The process took a full year, and now we invite you to join us on this journey.

Thank you for reading our stories and sharing moments of our lives with us. We hope you laughed a little, cried a little, found inspiration, unleashed your motivation, and learned some lessons that will serve you well. Living a life of success is a never-ending process. Congratulations on being on the road.

We are all committed to being the best we can be and leaving a lasting impact on the world where we spent some time. We invite you to join us in that commitment and connect with us further for resources, inspiration, motivation, and help to achieve your most tremendous success.

Connect with us and learn more about each
Life Lessons in Success author at:

🌐   LifeLessonsInSuccess.com

(f)   /LifeLessonsInSuccess

(y)   @lessons_success

(▶)   /LifeLessonsInSuccess

(in)   /Life-lessons-in-success

Will you post a review on Amazon? If you like what you read in *Life Lessons in Success*, I'd greatly appreciate it if you'd post a review on Amazon. This will help me reach more people. Thank you! Go here to post your review: www.lifelessonsinsuccess.com/bookreview

Made in the USA
Monee, IL
27 March 2021

63982769R00144